Use Your Heart

A Practical Guide to Loving Well

G.E. WILLIAMS

Dedication

To Valerie,
my wife and best friend.
You always try to use your heart to love me well, and for that I
am forever grateful.
Thanks for sharing this adventure with me.

Contents

Acknowledgments

I am grateful to Mary Shumard, who has been mentor and coach to me and my wife for many years, and has been invaluable in helping us to use our hearts to love one another well.

I am indebted to my colleague Mark Lutz for teaching me both the importance and the skill of listening with empathy. His consistent and relentless modeling and thorough training were critical in helping me learn how to connect with other people's hearts.

The overall structure of this book and the two following volumes owes much to two sources. The first is the book *Changes that Heal* by Dr. Henry Cloud. In it he outlines the four developmental tasks we need to complete to become healthy adults and the barriers that we face in achieving them. This book was foundational in helping me understand many personal and relational struggles.

I was introduced to the second source one day when I was in Mary's office and she showed me page 82 of *Listening for Heaven's Sake,* by Dr. Gary Sweeten, Dave Ping and Anne Clippard. The page was a diagram of the four building blocks of a therapeutic relationship, but she suggested that if I added the concept of reciprocity it would be a good general guideline for helping me to build better friendships as well. I put a Xeroxed copy of that page on my bathroom mirror and reflected on it daily for many years.

The structure for the three stages that I talk about in *How to Use Your Heart* is in many ways a synthesis of what I learned from the four building blocks and the four developmental tasks. The content of the three stages has many other important influences as well. I have learned much from the many books of Dr. Patrick Carnes, particularly from his *A Gentle Path through the Twelve Steps.* I have also been greatly influenced by Carl Rogers' book *On Becoming a Person: A Therapist's View of*

Psychotherapy. And, along with *Changes that Heal*, I have been impacted by the many books that Dr. Henry Cloud and Dr. John Townsend have written together.

I could never have written this book without the help and support of all the gang at Mosaic, a little house church in Dayton, Ohio. Thanks are due especially to Scott and Robyn, Bobby and Megan, Janet, Gian, Tim, Cindy and Val for the five years we spent together honing this material and practicing it together. Their ideas, input, feedback and genuine attempts to get better at using their hearts to love well were essential in the formation of this material.

I would not be who I am if it weren't for the opportunity that I had to manage a training store for Wendy's International for several years. Working with the guidance and encouragement of Amy Kessling and Ben Smith, I was able to spend most of my time training other managers. Here I learned that one of my unique passions was to take complicated tasks and break them into bite size, doable, repeatable behaviors that would help someone develop proficiency quickly. The main impetus for writing this book has been a desire to help people learn the specific skill sets required to love well, and to do it as quickly as possible.

Finally, I am very thankful to Lee Leonard for all his time and attention editing this book. I am deeply appreciative of his generosity in lending his expertise to this project.

Preface

I'm writing this book for everyone who wants to learn how to love people well and create meaningful relationships.

I'm writing for teens who are trying to figure out their way in the world, trying to learn the ropes of how to love and how to get love, and trying to figure out who they are and what they value. I sincerely hope that this book will help them be great friends and find great friends more quickly, and avoid the kind of relationships that can do great damage.

I'm writing for young married couples who are genuinely in love but find that they keep ending up in the same fights, the same confusion and disconnection, and who are wondering if perhaps they made a mistake. I'm writing for couples who have been married for a while and have drifted into settling for a marriage that is not what they had dreamed it would be. My desire is that you find hope in what is written here and that you learn how to talk to one another in ways that are deeply connecting and that restore and ignite the love you have for each other, and that in learning to love well you help each other to become all that you hope to be.

I'm writing this for people who long to find a romantic partner, a best friend, or a group of friends that they can share their life with, but who have been unable to do this and perhaps have even given up hope. I believe that what you long for can be achieved and that there are real changes you can make to put yourself in the position to help this happen. I have seen people who are lonely, frustrated, and even despondent put these principles into practice and find wonderful friends and lovers more quickly than they believed possible.

I'm writing this for men and women who want to make a positive impact on the lives of people they work with and create strong partnerships in their professional lives. A lot of great stuff has been written in the past decade or two about the importance of emotional intelligence and emotional health in the workplace, and I believe that learning the skills and principles in this book will help you grow your emotional capacity and accelerate your career.

I'm writing this for parents who want to give their children the best start in life. The best way to do this is to love them well and connect with them deeply. This isn't as easy as it sounds, and becomes immensely more complex as they enter their teen years. If you are just starting your journey as a parent, or if you have hit a roadblock with your son or daughter that feels insurmountable, I hope that you find in these pages a roadmap to a close and significant relationship.

Finally, I'm writing this for churches that want to learn how to be communities where loving, significant friendships can grow and flourish. If you are reading this and are not a follower of Christ I want to respect that you are coming to this topic with a completely different perspective on life. I think one of the things that keeps us from loving well is demonizing and caricaturing people who think differently than us (more on this in the section on Protecting Others' Power). I sincerely believe that you can get a lot out of this book. The principles that govern healthy relationships, and the skills required to love well, are the same regardless of your world view. We all desire to be loving spouses, parents and friends. I will try to do my best to be respectful that many readers will come with a different set of beliefs. But from time to time I will apply what I am talking about specifically to how it can impact the health of churches. I will do this because of a sincere and personal conviction that what Jesus wants most from his followers is to be a people who love others well, and that loving others well is something that churches have not always excelled in.

What Matters Most

Once Jesus was asked which was the greatest commandment. This is definitely a "what matters most" kind of question. There are hundreds of commandments in the Old Testament, so he had quite a selection to choose from. You might be familiar with his answer:

Jesus replied: "'Love the Lord your God with all your heart and with all your soul and with all your mind.' This is the first and greatest commandment." (Matthew 22:37, 38)

But it is fascinating that Jesus didn't stop there. In his mind the answer was incomplete. And so he continues:

"And the second is like it: 'Love your neighbor as yourself.'" (Matthew 22:39)

Why does he do this? Why does he give a bonus answer? And why stop there? Why not name the top three commandments? Or the top seven? We are not left to speculate, because he goes on to say:

"All the Law and the Prophets hang on these two commandments." (Matthew 22:40)

In Jesus' mind these two commands are inseparable because they form the core of everything else God talks about in the law and the prophets. In essence, everything else God revealed in the law and the prophets is there to help us understand what it means to love; and how to love God and love our neighbor as we love ourselves. Everything hangs on these two commands. Take away these two commands and everything else falls apart – they no longer have any meaning. What really matters to God is that we grow in our capacity to give and receive love in our relationship with him and with our neighbors.

And then, on the night that Jesus was betrayed and arrested, he upped the ante. He gave what he called a *new* commandment:

"A new command I give you: Love one another. As I have

loved you, so you must love one another." (John 13:34)

At first glance this might not seem like a new command, but a restatement of the second greatest commandment (to love our neighbors). But it was new because it had a more defined audience - other Christ followers; and because it had a new standard – to love in the same way that we are loved by Jesus. And then, to make sure his disciples understood that this was another "what matters most moment," he added

"By this everyone will know that you are my disciples, if you love one another." (John 13:35)

Here Jesus states that the single identifying characteristic of his followers is their capacity to love other Christians in the same way He loves them. It is a high standard and one that helps bring focus. What Jesus wanted most from his followers was to create a community where love would be so deep and constant that anybody looking at this community, whether from the inside or the outside, would be struck mostly by the quality of the love.

From these statements of Jesus it is clear that he believes that what really matters is that we grow in our capacity to give and receive love in our relationship with him, with our neighbors, with ourselves, and with other Christ followers.

Paul, an early and influential follower of Jesus, hammers this same point home. He reminds us that, though the Christian life has a lot of different facets to it, at the heart of everything is growing in our capacity to love:

If I speak in the tongues of men or of angels, but do not have love, I am only a resounding gong or a clanging cymbal. If I have the gift of prophecy and can fathom all mysteries and all knowledge, and if I have a faith that can move mountains, but do not have love, I am nothing. If I give all I possess to the poor and give over my body to hardship that I may boast, but do not have love, I gain nothing. (1 Corinthians 13:1-3)

If you want a way to gauge your spiritual growth, says Paul, this is how you can do it: evaluate your capacity to give and receive love. What is the strength and depth of your love relationships with God, others and with yourself? That is all that really matters – everything else hangs on this.

But here is the problem: Creating and building love relationships is hard work. It is often painful work. It is often confusing work. And there are a lot of things that we can do that are much easier than building love relationships. And so, little by little, we turn relationship into religion – a set of doctrinal beliefs that we can memorize and defend and argue about. Or we turn relationship into ritual – a set of routines that we can practice over and over again without having to even make eye contact with other people, let alone learn how to love them. Or we turn relationships into programs – a set of goals that we can budget for and staff towards without having to learn how to love well. I don't think there is anything wrong with programs or rituals or defining one's doctrinal beliefs. The problem is when they become a substitution for doing the hard work of loving one another. When that happens they are just a resounding gong or a clanging cymbal.

The Church has been known for various things at various times over its two-thousand year history. At times it has been known for its political power. At times it has been known for its social impact in starting things like universities and orphanages and hospitals. At times it has been known for its moral corruption. At times it has been known for its intolerance and cruelty towards people of other faiths. At times it has been known for its generosity, and at other times it has been known for hoarding financial riches while poor people starve. Whatever the Church's reputation at any point in history, it has usually earned it. I believe the church is never more beautiful, and never more what Jesus envisioned and intended for it be, than when it is known for its capacity to deeply love those both inside and outside of its fellowship. That seems to be what the Church of the first century was known for, and I believe the Holy Spirit is leading the church into a season where we reclaim our birthright as adopted sons and daughters of God, and followers of His son, and become known primarily as a community of deep and abiding love relationships.

If you are a leader in the church in any capacity, let me ask you this: Is there anything you could focus on that would make your church more beautiful to God than to help your members love well and love deeply? To become a church that is known for loving the marginalized, loving its enemies, loving one another, and loving God? To be a church where husbands and wives learn how to love one another, and where parents learn how to love their children well?

Most Christians understand, at least on a theoretical level, the importance of love. But we often struggle with the specific steps to take and the specific skills to practice to become a more loving person. Often in our attempts to relate with others we come across as arrogant, rude, judgmental, and disrespectful. In my own life I became aware of the centrality of love to the Christian life several decades ago, and yet I have spent most of my life woefully inadequate at being able to love well the people closest to me, let alone strangers and even (as Christ commands) my enemies. But I have been captivated by a vision of a church that loves so deeply and so well that the world cannot help but take notice and even long to be part of such a community. So I have spent much of my adult life trying to figure out why I inadvertently harm the people I'm trying to love, why they harm me when they are trying to love me, how to love them better, and how to teach others what it takes to love well and connect deeply. It is my hope that this book will be a useful tool towards that end.

Introduction

Above all else, guard your heart, for everything you do flows from it.
Proverbs 4:23

Here is our hearts' dilemma: The greatest joy, meaning and satisfaction in life come from our relationships with others; and the greatest pain, wounding and scars in life also come from our relationships with others. We begin relationships, whether they are friendships, romance, parenting or business relationships, with high hopes. Yet we don't have to think very hard to remember times when those high hopes fizzled out or, worse, turned to devastation.

So how do we guard our heart? Sometimes we try to guard it by withdrawing from relationship altogether. And yet that can lead to loneliness and depression that is just as debilitating as the pain of destructive relationships. In attempting to guard our hearts we starve our hearts.

Is it possible to increase the healthy, life-giving friendships in our lives while minimizing the relationships that harm us? Is it possible to know the steps to take to turn struggling and stagnant relationships into thriving friendships? Is it possible to move beyond the roll of the dice "I hope this relationship works" mentality and move to a place where you are confident in your own ability to begin and nurture great friendships?

I believe it is. This book is the first of a series of three books whose purpose is to help you learn how to use your heart so that you can love others well, and experience deep and satisfying connection with the people in your life; while learning to avoid the kinds of relationships that drain and harm your heart. In order for you to do this there are four things you need to master:

- **Understanding the three stages**: There are three stages in building a healthy relationship. In order to have confidence in our own ability to create satisfying friendships, we need to understand the importance of each stage, how to enjoy it instead of rushing through it, and how to successfully navigate to the next stage. This book, *How to Use Your Heart: A Practical Guide to Loving Well*, focuses on the first stage. The second and third volumes in this series, *How to Use Your Heart: A Practical Guide to Connecting Deeply* and *How to Use Your Heart: A Practical Guide to Sharing the Journey* will cover the second and third stages respectively.

- **Relationship skills**: Each stage has its own set of critical skills that are absolutely necessary in order to love well, and yet most of us have never been taught these skills. Becoming proficient in each of these skills is *the most important thing we can do* to increase our ability to form great friendships. That is why much of this book is focused on learning and practicing these skills. Just as you cannot learn to play the piano or shoot free-throws without practicing, you cannot learn to be a great friend, parent or spouse without practicing.

- **Improve your people-picker:** Besides improving your own ability to create great friendships, you need to be able to recognize when other people have this ability (or at least are willing to learn and work towards it) and when they don't. If not, you could spend years investing in a relationship and still get nowhere. This series will help you understand the red flags to watch out for when picking people to be in relationship with.

- **Avoid the detours:** there are certain relationship patterns that we can fall into even with people that we love and who love us, that can get us stuck in a relational swamp for years, or even decades. By knowing what these detours look like we can avoid them and save ourselves years of misery.

The Three Stages: the road ahead and where this book fits in

This book series is divided into three volumes, each of which will help you understand what is critical for that stage of building a relationship, and will also teach you the skills you need to thrive in that stage of relationship building.

Stage One: Two Separate, Valuable and Powerful People

For a relationship between two people to be life-giving each person needs to have a sense of their own value and power, and each needs to respect the other's value and power. This means each person is allowed to have their own wants, needs, emotions, thoughts, opinions and values. If you are in a relationship where you need to continually give up or hide your own opinion or values or emotions in order to be accepted, then you have lost your value and power. If you are in a relationship where the other person cannot express their wants or values or ideas then they have lost their value and power. Unfortunately, we have all learned a myriad of subtle ways to disempower one another, even people we are trying to love. Most of the time we don't even know that this is happening: we just have a vague, unsettled feeling in the pit of our stomachs that we learn to ignore, thinking that it's just one of the prices to pay to have friendship.

In stage one we are going to examine how your heart works, and how you can use your heart to discover your own value and power, and also how you can use your heart to respect and nurture other people's value and power. The skills we will learn and practice in this first book are the most important skills to master if you want to love others well.

Stage Two: Creating Connection

For our hearts to thrive we need a sense of being connected with other people. Some of these connections will be light and brief, and some will be deep and enduring, but they are all important. In stage two we will discover the steps that you can take to begin building connection with other people. We'll talk about the risks involved and how you can minimize them so that connecting becomes a safer experience, and we'll practice the key skills needed to build stronger and stronger connections.

For a lot of us getting close to and connected with others can seem mysterious. We know it when we see it in others, we long for it, but we just don't know how to get there. We see other couples who seem deeply connected, we see other managers at work that have great relationships with their employees, we know acquaintances who seem to have a real sense of belonging with others – we just don't know how they do it. We may conclude they were lucky enough to find the right person, or that they have the right personality type. Along with this comes the idea that we are not lucky and we have the wrong personality.

I promise you that luck and personality have nothing to do with it. In *How to Use Your Heart: A Guide to Connecting Deeply* we will take the mystery out of creating connection and give you the tools you need to go into each day with the power to create connection with the people who are important to you.

Stage Three: Sharing the journey

Every once in a while you will have a Stage Two relationship that you want to take to another level, and you realize it is time to have "the talk." This may happen after months of dating when you begin to wonder if this person could be "the one." It may happen when you decide you want to start a new business and there is a colleague you want to talk to about becoming your partner. It may happen when you notice someone at work who is strong in an area you want to grow in and you want to ask them to mentor you. It may happen as your child grows and it's time to talk about them expanding their responsibilities around the house. It may happen when you are put in charge of a team at work and you need to accomplish a strategic goal together.

In other words, there is somewhere you want to go in life, and you want to ask someone to take the journey with you. You need to know if they want to go to the same place, how fast they want to travel, if they are willing to pay the price to get there, and who will be responsible for what on the trip. We also need to learn how to have the hard conversations that help us stay on track, but have them in a way that builds trust and connection. Just as importantly, we need to learn to recognize when someone simply doesn't want to do the work to stay on track; and we need to discover this early in the relationship building process, before we invest our life savings in opening a business together or invest our lives in marriage. This will be the focus of the last book in this series: *How to Use Your Heart: A Practical Guide to Sharing the Journey.*

Before we begin, there are four things that are important to understand about working through the three stages of relationship.

We must go through the three stages in order

One of the biggest reasons we have had relationships that have not been life giving is we have gone through the relationship building process out of order. We try to create connection (Stage Two) before we have discovered if the other person is able to respect and value us as a separate person (Stage One), and then end up in one-sided relationships where it seems we are doing all the work with little or no pay-off. Or we make relational commitments to people (Stage Three) before we have built a strong connection with them (Stage Two) and find that we are connected at the hip with someone who is very different from who we imagined them to be.

One of the common mistakes I see in people whom I am coaching in their dating relationships is that they show up for the first date with Stage Three on their mind. They are not trying to establish a foundation of respect and value, nor are they paying attention to whether or not their date has the ability to treat them as a separate person. Instead they are wondering whether or not this is someone they can marry: Do they have the right income? Do they want to have kids? Do they want to date one person exclusively?

There are a couple reasons this is a problem. The first is that it puts way too much pressure on a first date. It puts the weight of my future and my most important hopes and dreams on date one. I find a common theme with men and women who approach dating in this way is that they hate dating. It's too stressful. The second problem is if someone does seem to match the profile of what we are looking for on the first date then we let our hearts run away and create romantic images of a wedding and married life, and we don't even know if they have the ability to respect us or the ability to create and nurture connection, or the ability to build trust by keeping promises.

Whatever the relationship, it is essential that we go through the stages step by step.

You have to be able to love people well before you can connect with them deeply, and you have to be able to create connection with people before you can make healthy and realistic commitments to sharing life together.

Only advance to the next stage when there is reciprocity on the current stage

This means that you only move on to Stage Two when *both people in the relationship* are able to love well. Only move on to Stage Three when *both people in the relationship* show an ability and desire to create connection. Sometimes we think that if we invest more in a relationship than the other person, they will eventually take the relationship more seriously and someday catch up with us ("I know he *says* he doesn't want to get married, but if I'm the perfect girlfriend I know I can change his mind!"). This doesn't work, and it puts us in a place where we are doing most of the work in a relationship (without being asked) and not getting the payoff we desire.

If you approach relationship building with the idea that it is your job to get someone to fall in love with you, or it is your job to get someone to want to be your friend, then you will feel powerless, frustrated and eventually will give up. There is no way you can have this kind of control over other people.

What you can do, however, is treat other people in a way that you protect their value and power as individuals, and *pay attention* to which people are treating you the same way in return. You can then begin to create connection with these people and *pay attention* to who is also trying to create a connection with you. These are the relationships in which you want to invest more time and energy. Then, from this group, you will begin inviting people into Stage Three and you will *pay attention* to the energy and enthusiasm they bring to the idea of sharing the journey with you, and if they are willing to grow and change in order to keep their commitments. When their enthusiasm and commitment to growth is the same as yours, then you have found the people that you want to let into the deep places of your heart. These are people that you want as best friends, as mentors, as a spouse, or as a business partner.

You don't have to bet the farm. You don't have to set yourself up to be heartbroken. At each stage you only take the risks that are appropriate for that stage.

Each stage builds on the previous stage; it doesn't replace the previous stage

In Stage One, we focus on paying attention that there are two separate, valuable, powerful people in the relationship. In Stage Two, though we are now focusing on building connection, it is important to remember that we are building connection between two separate, valuable, powerful people. In Stage Three, though we are now focusing on sharing life together through having shared agreements, it is critical to remember that this sharing is happening between two separate, valuable, powerful people who are building connection together. Each stage builds on the others, and the moment you stop doing the work of the previous stages the relationship begins to unravel.

It's never too late to go through the three stages and create a great partnership

If you are in a relationship that is not working the way you dreamed it would and need to either get unstuck or do some repair work, it is likely that you skipped a step or two and need to go back and lay a new foundation. By working through the steps and learning the critical skills together, relationships that are struggling and debilitating can begin to flourish and become all that you hoped for and more.

One final word of introduction just to be clear: Not all good relationships need to get to Stage Three. Some of my favorite people are friends that I meet up with at the local sports bar to watch sports and play trivia. We all come from different backgrounds and have very different views on life, but we have a fun time connecting over the Ohio State Buckeyes, the Cincinnati Reds and Bengals, and the topics of whatever trivia game we are currently playing. They even tolerate my fanatical love of the Los Angeles Lakers. While all this is happening we talk about work and kids and hobbies and vacations and whatever else is going on in life. It's a great Stage Two friendship that has no reason to go on to Stage Three. People show up when they want and stay as long as they want and participate as much as they want. The formal commitments, shared goals and guidelines that are part of Stage Three have no place in this kind of relationship and would actually take away from the fun.

Part One:

Living With Your Heart Alive

1 How Your Heart Works: Emotions (Part 1)

If you want to love well and connect deeply then you need to understand how your heart works. And a good place to start in understanding how your heart works is to understand your emotions and what your emotions are trying to tell you.

Most of us have no idea what our emotions are telling us. Our basic view of emotions is that happy emotions are pleasant and good and should be sought out, and emotions like fear, anger and sadness are painful and bad and should be avoided. And so we spend a lot of time trying to create happy feelings, and we also put a lot of energy into avoiding or ignoring painful feelings.

While this may be the predominant response to emotions in our culture, it is wholly inadequate for helping us to love well. In fact, it is certain to prevent us from learning how to love well because our emotions are always tied to the people and things we love.

Love machine

You are a love machine. You were created to love. It is how you were designed. You were created to love God, to love others, and to love yourself. It's how you are wired. You love your pets; you love your hobbies. If you don't love your career, then you probably long for a career that you would love. You even love things. If you own a Harley-Davidson, you probably love it. If you are a sports fan, you don't just like your favorite team, you love them. It's just the way you were made.

And that is where emotions come in. Here is the most important thing you need to understand about your emotions. When you get this, you are on your way to learning how to love yourself and love others more deeply:

Your emotions are signals that let you know the current state of connection with the people and things you love.

In this chapter I want to look at our four primary emotions: happiness, anger, fear, and sadness.[1] Each of these emotions tells us something critical about our relationship with something we love. By the way, if you are one of those people who are uncomfortable with "touchy-feely" things this should be some comfort to you: the purpose of being aware of your emotions is not so that you can wallow in them (more on that later). The purpose of being aware of your emotions is so that you know what to do to protect and strengthen your relationship with the people and things you love.

Happiness

Happiness is a signal of a *strong connection* in our love relationship. Happiness means that everything is going well in our relationship with someone or something we love. It can be a sign that we feel close, or a sign that the person we love is doing well. Look at these examples of happy feelings:

We feel playful when we are wrestling with our toddler.
We feel proud of ourselves after successfully completing a major project at work.
We feel delighted when our husband sends us flowers at work.
We feel ecstatic when our team wins the championship.
We feel euphoric when we hear that our best friend just got engaged.
We feel overjoyed at the birth of our child.

As you can see from the examples above, sometimes our

happy feelings can be intense and other times they can be mild. The feeling may be brief or it may last a while. But it always is a sign that something is going well in a relationship that is important to us.

Anger

Anger and *fear* are twin emotions. They each signal that something we love is being *threatened*, but each responds to the threat in a different way.

Anger is a sign that something we love is being threatened and that it would be best to *move towards the threat*, seeking to eliminate it. Look at these examples of anger:

We feel irked when someone is thirty minutes late (again) and we might miss the movie we planned on seeing.

We feel frustrated when our children don't put their toys away.

We feel steamed when our character is maligned.

We feel outraged when we see someone treated unjustly.

We feel irate when we discover that our child is being bullied at school.

As we think about our anger it is important to distinguish between our *feelings* and our *behaviors*. For some of us, anger has always been associated with destructive and frightening behaviors, such as slamming doors, screaming, or even physical violence. When this happens we tend to think of anger as a bad or dangerous emotion and something it would be better to not feel.

This is unfortunate. Anger is a critical emotion since it is a signal that we need to guard and protect something we love. If our child is being bullied, we need to feel our anger; it lets us know we need to meet immediately with school officials and put a stop to the bullying. If someone is consistently late we need to feel our anger; it lets us know that we are being disrespected and that we need to have a conversation with our friend. When we don't pay attention to our anger we tend to tolerate behavior that will eventually cause us to lose our relationship with people and things we love.

Fear

As with anger, fear is also a sign that something we love is being threatened, but fear warns us it would be best to *move away from the threat*, seeking to escape or minimize the damage caused by it:

We feel cautious when driving on icy roads.
We feel nervous when we know there are going to be layoffs at work.
We feel apprehensive when asked out on a date by someone whose character we don't trust.
We feel alarmed when a supervisor threatens to fire us unless we keep quiet about an illegal activity.
We feel terrified when we see an out of control car careening our direction.

Fear is another critical emotion that we often do not allow ourselves to experience. Sometimes fear is viewed as a sign of weakness or cowardice; it's a feeling for babies and little children but not for strong adults. The problem with ignoring fear is it often leads to ignoring real danger. In his book *The Gift of Fear* Gavin De Becker relates story after story of people who ignored their feelings of fear, telling themselves they were being silly or childish, and suffered great harm in situations where the danger was completely avoidable.

There are times when we need to be angry and confront something that is threatening us, but there are other times where we need to be afraid and move away from the threat in order to protect ourselves or those that we love.

Sadness

Sadness is a signal that we have *lost* something that we love.

We feel glum when our favorite TV show is cancelled.

We feel melancholy when it rains and our barbecue is cancelled.

We feel discouraged when it seems that God is not answering our prayers.

We feel crushed when our girlfriend breaks up with us.

We feel devastated when someone close to us dies.

Sadness is another emotion that we have difficulty feeling and paying attention to. Sadness is important because it tells us that a connection to something that we love no longer exists, and we need to let go and grieve. If we don't let go and grieve, we get stuck in a past that no longer exists, and our hearts are less able to connect with something good and real in the present. If our girlfriend breaks up with us, we need to grieve and let go so we can eventually move on and connect with someone else. If God has not been answering our prayers the way we would like, we need to grieve and let go of the idea that God will always give us what we want so that we can have a healthy relationship with the real God who sometimes says "no" or "not yet." As with the other emotions, sometimes the sadness is brief and minor, and at other times the sadness is lasting and intense, depending on the depth of the connection and the importance of the relationship.

Living with your heart fully alive

If you want to love well and connect deeply you need to learn how to live with your heart fully alive, and how to help others to live with their hearts fully alive.

Sometimes we think that our goal is to feel good and to help others feel good. When this happens we ignore, deny, and even medicate painful feelings. The problem with this approach is that your heart functions like one master dimmer switch. If you turn down the anger button you will feel less angry, but you will also turn down your capacity to feel all the other feelings as well. On the other hand, when we allow ourselves to feel our painful feelings deeply, we are also able to feel happy feelings deeply as well. So I want to suggest a new goal when it comes to feeling your feelings:

> ***Instead of trying to feel good, try to feel deeply.***

You may be thinking "Wait a minute! I thought you said we don't have to wallow in our emotions! Feeling deeply sounds like wallowing!" Hang in there with me for a moment.

Here is the point I'm trying to make, and it is an extremely important point to settle before moving forward: Because our emotions are signals of the current state of connection with the people and things we love, the deeper the connection the deeper the emotion will be. If a stranger cuts in front of you in line at Burger King that would be disrespectful and you might feel a little angry (after all, you don't know him, he's probably either a jerk or was unaware of what he was doing, and all you lost was 45 seconds); but if someone at work lied and blamed a costly error on your work, that would also be disrespectful – but this time you might feel intensely angry (what is at stake is your reputation as a professional as well as your income). In the first case the minor anger is a signal to do nothing and let it go; in the second case the intense anger is a signal to react as swiftly and completely as you need to protect your reputation and income. So, even with intense emotions the point is not to wallow in them, but to take the intensity as a signal that there is something very important at stake and to react accordingly.

So how deeply do we need to feel? That will depend on two things. First, it will depend on how much you love the person, experience or thing the emotion is about. The sadness you feel when a close friend dies will be much deeper than the sadness you feel when your favorite celebrity dies. Secondly, it will depend on the degree of change in the relationship with the person or thing that you love. You will feel more deeply angry when you discover that your spouse has been lying to you than you will when you discover that your spouse misplaced your car keys, because lying creates a much bigger change in the relationship.

Practice Session: Paying attention to your heart

Let's do some basic exercises to help you understand your own heart. The more you practice being aware of what is going on in your heart, the more you will understand the current state of your relationships with all the people and things you love in life. Please don't skip this session. The practice sessions in this book are the most important parts because this is where you will develop the skills you need to love well.

Complete the following self-reflection exercises. It is important that you don't evaluate your feelings at this point. Don't try to judge whether or not you *should* have felt that feeling. You are just trying to understand your heart at this point.

Happiness

What was one of the times in your childhood when you felt the most happy? What did this happiness say about your connection with someone or something you loved?

What was one of the times in the past year when you felt the most happy? What did this happiness say about your connection with someone or something you loved?

What was a time this past week when you felt happy? What did this happiness say about your connection with someone or something you loved?

Anger

What was one of the times in your childhood when you felt the angriest? What did this anger say about your connection with someone or something you loved?

What was one of the times in the past year when you felt the angriest? What did this anger say about your connection with someone or something you loved?

What was a time this past week when you felt angry? What did this anger say about your connection with someone or something you loved?

Fear

What was one of the times in your childhood when you felt the most afraid? What did this fear say about your connection with someone or something you loved?

What was one of the times in the past year when you felt the most afraid? What did this fear say about your connection with someone or something you loved?

What was a time this past week when you felt afraid? What did this fear say about your connection with someone or something you loved?

Of the four emotions talked about in this chapter, which is the hardest for you to allow yourself to feel? Which is the easiest? Why do you think that is?

2 How Your Heart Works: Emotions (Part 2)

In this chapter we are going to look at four secondary emotions. Just as with the primary emotions, each of these emotions tells us something critical about our relationship with something we love:

Guilt

Guilt is a signal that *our actions have compromised* a love relationship. Look at these examples of guilt:

We feel sorry when we show up late for a date.
We feel regret when we have lied to a friend.
We feel remorseful when we have screamed at our children.
We feel devastated when we realize that our addiction has caused untold harm to our family.

Guilt lets us know that our behavior has damaged a relationship and that we need to do some repair work. We need to sincerely apologize. We may need to make amends. In some circumstances, we may need to confess our behavior because the person we are in relationship with doesn't know we have harmed the relationship.

Guilt is a difficult feeling for us to feel and so we try to ignore it. We try to pretend that our actions are no big deal and that the relationship is fine. We know that if we take responsibility for our behavior and confess what we have done that it would radically change the other person's perception of the relationship, at least for a season. So we pretend everything is okay. The problem with pretend relationships is that they never satisfy our hearts.

Shame

Shame is a signal that we believe *our worth* as someone to love has been *compromised:*

We feel self-conscious when trying on a new bathing suit.

We feel embarrassed when we lose our temper in front of co-workers.

We feel humiliated when our spouse talks about one of our private struggles publicly without our permission.

We feel defiled and degraded when we have been sexually abused.

We often confuse shame and guilt, but in reality they are very different. Guilt is about my behavior, whereas shame is about my worth as a person. Guilt says I have hurt a love relationship, but shame says I am not worth loving. Sometimes we feel that we are not worth loving because of something we have done, and sometimes we feel we are not worth loving because of something that has been done to us. Either way, shame builds a wall around our hearts and prevents us from being connected with God and others. Because of this, shame can be a very painful emotion.

The only productive purpose of shame is to make us aware that somehow we have adopted the false view that we are not worth being loved, so that we can correct that belief and get back to a place of connection with God and others. If we ignore our feelings of shame, we will not do the work of figuring out what lies about our self-worth we have accepted as truth and will continue to hide our real selves from others, either by isolating or by pretending to be someone we are not.

Confusion

Confusion is a signal that something might change or has changed in a love relationship, but we are *not sure what the change is or will be, or how intense the change is or will be.*

We feel uncertain about whether or not to sell our grandmother's necklace that we inherited.

We feel perplexed when a usually friendly co-worker says

something sarcastic to us on his way out the door.

We feel bewildered when a close friend withdraws from the relationship with no explanation.

We feel torn when we are deciding whether or not to accept a great new job that will mean moving to a new town, severing great friendships for us and our children.

Sometimes emotional confusion is merely a result of intellectual confusion. If we don't know whether or not someone's statement was sincere or sarcastic then we are not sure whether to feel honored or insulted. But there are times when we feel no intellectual confusion but we still feel emotional confusion. This is because one event can be connected to our heart in several different ways, connected to several different things that we love. And sometimes the first and most intense emotional response is not the deepest and most significant response. If I am at a new car dealership thinking about buying my dream car, I could feel ecstatic about the idea of owning the car, and at the same time have an underlying sense of worry about agreeing to such a large monthly payment. Sometimes these underlying feelings, though not as intense at the moment, are the ones that are most significant.

When we feel confused it is a signal to slow down and explore these different connections before moving on. For some of us, however, confusion is such an uncomfortable experience that we react to an event or make a decision quickly not because it is the best reaction or decision, but because we want to escape the discomfort of uncertainty.

Loneliness

Loneliness is a signal that we are missing a love relationship that we were designed to have.

We feel left-out when we hear about a party to which we were not invited.

We feel ignored when our siblings receive attention and affection from our parents and we do not.

We feel isolated when we move to a new city and after eight months have not been able to build any friendships.

We feel uncherished when we long to be married but have no romantic relationship.

We feel estranged when we have no family or community to which we have a sense of belonging.

We feel desolate when we continue in a state of isolation for a long period of time.

Since we were created to be in deep and significant love relationships with God and others, loneliness is a signal that something has gone very wrong. It is a signal that we need to identify what relationship is missing and take steps to find and build that relationship. Many of us ignore our feelings of loneliness, however. Sometimes we ignore them because of shame (we believe we are not worthy of being loved so loneliness is our only option). Sometimes we ignore them because we don't know how to build healthy relationships, and so have no hope of getting the friendships we need. And sometimes we don't trust ourselves to choose the right people to be in relationship with (we've been hurt before and loneliness, at least at first, seems like the lesser of two evils).

Practice Session: Paying attention to your heart

Again, let's do some basic exercises to help you understand your own heart. The more you practice being aware of what is going on in your heart, the more you will understand the current state of your relationships with all the people and things you love in life.

Complete the following self-reflection exercises. It is important that you don't evaluate your feelings at this point. Don't try to judge whether or not you *should* have felt that feeling. You are just trying to understand your heart at this point.

Guilt

What was one of the times in your childhood when you felt the most guilt? What did this guilt say about your connection with someone or something you loved?

What was one of the times in the past year when you felt the most guilt? What did this guilt say about your connection with someone or something you loved?

What was a time this past week when you felt guilt? What did this guilt say about your connection with someone or something you loved?

Shame

What was one of the times in your childhood when you felt the most shame? What did this shame say about your connection with someone or something you loved?

What was one of the times in the past year when you felt the most shame? What did this shame say about your connection with someone or something you loved?

What was a time this past week when you felt shame? What did this shame say about your connection with someone or something you loved?

Confused

What was one of the times in your childhood when you felt the most confused? What did this confusion say about your connection with someone or something you loved?

What was one of the times in the past year when you felt the most confused? What did this confusion say about your connection with someone or something you loved?

What was a time this past week when you felt confused? What did this confusion say about your connection with someone or something you loved?

Loneliness

What was one of the times in your childhood when you felt the loneliest? What did this loneliness say about your connection with someone or something you loved?

What was one of the times in the past year when you felt the loneliest? What did this loneliness say about your connection with someone or something you loved?

What was a time this past week when you felt lonely? What did this loneliness say about your connection with someone or something you loved?

Of the four emotions in this section, which emotion is the hardest for you to allow yourself to feel? Which is the easiest? Why do you think that is?

3 Invalidating Emotions

We have seen how our emotions allow us to understand what is happening in our relationship with the people and things we love. And yet the reality is that most of us have been taught to ignore or distrust our emotions for most of our lives. The primary reason we do this is because our emotions have been invalidated, and in turn we have learned to invalidate our own emotions and also those of the people we are trying to love.

We invalidate someone's emotions whenever we give them the impression that what they are feeling is the wrong way to feel at that moment. Take a look at the following ways we invalidate one another, and notice how rampant a practice this is. Notice how many of these phrases:

- Were regularly used by your parents or other authority figures.
- Are regularly used by people you are in relationship with right now.
- You have used in just the past week.

Examples of Invalidation

Invalidating sadness

Cheer up, it's not so bad.
Get over it.
Don't be sad.
Don't be so sad.
Let me see that smile.
Stop crying.
If you don't stop crying I'll give you something to cry about.
Stop being such a baby.
Suck it up.

If that's the worst thing that happens to you then you're lucky.

Why are you always whining?

It's not that big of a deal.

You're way too sensitive.

Did the little baby get his feelings hurt?

Remember, God causes all things to work together for good for those who love Him.

Where's your faith?

Look on the bright side.

You're better off without...(him, her, that job, etc.)

There are plenty of fish in the sea.

You're just feeling sorry for yourself.

No one said life was a bed of roses.

You should feel thankful for what you have.

After all I've done for you, you're going to sit there and cry?

You are such a Debbie downer.

Don't be an Eeyore.

Invalidating anger

Chill out.

Take a chill pill.

Watch your temper.

Don't blow a gasket.

Calm down.

Don't take it so personally.

I was only joking.

What's your problem?

Act like an adult.

Control yourself.

Don't get angry.

Don't get *that* angry.

She didn't mean that the way you are taking it.
Someone woke up on the wrong side of the bed this morning!
What's your problem?
No one else gets angry when I do that.
Let's look at this rationally.

Invalidating fear

There's no need to be afraid.
Stop being such a scaredy-cat.
Grow up.
Man up.
Stop acting like a baby.
You're being irrational.
It's time to put on your big boy pants.
Stop being such a coward.
There's nothing to be afraid of.
It's not *that* scary.
Why would you let a little thing like that scare you?
Are you a chicken?
No one else is afraid.
You just want attention.
Did someone tell you that life was supposed to be easy?
What's your problem?
What's your problem this time?
Stop making a scene.
Just deal with it.
Stop being such a drama queen.
You've got to be kidding me!
My five year old cousin isn't afraid of *that!*
You should feel excited, not scared.
You should feel lucky for the opportunity.
You're making this much harder than it really is.

Invalidating guilt

Everybody does it.
What they don't know won't hurt them.
What's the big deal?
Just ignore it.
Forget about it.
Don't take yourself so seriously.
Don't get so bent out of shape.
Live a little.
Don't be such a killjoy.
You're making it worse than it really is.
It's not as bad as it seems.
You're over-thinking this.
You have an overactive conscience.
This is the twenty-first century; nobody gets bothered by that anymore.
One time won't hurt.

Invalidating shame

Don't be silly.
No one thinks that you are too…(fat, thin, tall, short, etc.)
No one notices your…(acne, bald spot, spare tire, etc.)
It's all in your head.
Stop being so self-obsessed.
You're making a mountain out of a molehill.
Let's all feel sorry for…
Get over yourself.
That's absurd.
But everybody loves you.
Do you ever think about anyone but yourself?
Nobody cares.

Let's think about this rationally.
He probably didn't mean to embarrass you.

Invalidating loneliness

There's someone out there for you.
Someday you'll understand.
You should feel thankful for what you have.
Let's look at what you *do* have.
Don't I count for anything?
But you have so many friends.
If you stop focusing on yourself you'll be much happier.
Don't worry. God has a plan.
You just need to pray more.
You don't need anyone.
You're going to look back and laugh about this.
That's life. Deal with it.
This is getting old.
Feeling sorry for yourself isn't going to help.
You're just not trying hard enough.
I'm playing my invisible violin for you.
I'm sure it will all work out.
Things will look better tomorrow.

Invalidating happiness

Don't look so superior.
What have you got to be so happy about?
Don't get so full of yourself.
Why are you smiling like that?
Who wound you up today?
What's gotten into you?
Why do you have that look on your face?

Don't be ridiculous.

Don't get excited.

Don't get so excited.

Wipe that smile of your face.

Don't count your chickens before they hatch.

Don't look so self-satisfied.

What drugs are you taking?

Oh, sorry, I thought you had something *really worth* being excited about.

That's all it takes to make you happy? You need to get a life.

That's nothing to make a big deal of.

I worry about you.

Who cares?

As you can see, there is an epidemic of invalidation in the world today. You would think that, since emotions always say something important about our relationship with the people and things we love, we would be very careful to pay attention to one another's emotions. Instead, we seem to go out of our way to let one another know that what we are feeling is the wrong thing to feel. And we are very creative in our invalidation. We tell each other what not to feel. We tell each other what we should be feeling instead. We tell each other that we are feeling too intensely. We tell each other that if we were smarter or had a better perspective we would feel something different. We resort to clichés, and we try to spiritualize away our need to feel our feelings. We tell each other that we are the only ones who react that way, and we even resort to belittling one another's emotions. It would almost be funny if the results weren't so devastating.

What happens when we invalidate

The first and most critical result of invalidation is it decreases our ability to love well. Think about it for a minute. If our emotions are signals about what is happening in a love relationship, when we tell someone not to feel a certain way we are inadvertently telling them to stop paying attention to the things they love. In fact, we are really telling them not to love so much. If a six year old is crying because a friend moved away and we tell him to "stop being such a baby", we are telling him "don't love your friends to the point that you feel sad when they go away." If a teenager who is furious because someone started a rumor about her, and we tell her to "settle down" or to "stop making a mountain out of molehill," we are really saying "don't love and respect yourself so much that you want to protect your reputation."

Another result of invalidation is that we learn to distrust our emotions. Instead of seeing them as important signals about what is going on in our hearts, we see them as weaknesses. We stop paying attention to our fear and walk into situations that are harmful to us. We ignore our anger and allow people to cross our boundaries. We disregard our guilt and continue to do things that destroy our relationships until it is too late.

Sometimes the result of invalidation is a heart with screwed-up wiring. Men, for example, are taught very early in life that feelings like sadness and fear are signs of weakness. Instead of being allowed to feel these vulnerable emotions and learn what they mean, little boys are told not to be "such a sissy." Constant invalidation teaches these boys that any vulnerable emotion should be translated immediately into anger, which is perceived as powerful and manly. In other homes anger is seen as the destructive emotion, and whenever someone gets angry they are told to "watch their temper." In such cases, we can sometimes rewire our anger so that it turns into fear, which is another emotion that tells us we need to protect the love relationship, but we end up hiding or withdrawing from a problem that is our responsibility to solve; or we rewire the emotion to turn into sadness, because we are not actively protecting the thing we love and assume it will be lost.

Having one or more of our emotions invalidated like this can have another impact: it lessens our ability to feel other emotions deeply. We have already talked about the reality that our heart functions as one master dimmer switch. We can respond to continuous invalidation by dimming our anger so that we are not aware of it, but the problem is we will also dim the other emotions, including happiness.

Another result of invalidation is that, since we have ignored or rewired the signal our heart is giving us, we don't attend to the real problem and it continues to fester. If we don't pay attention to our sadness we will not grieve the thing we have lost and the sadness will move underground and can turn into depression. We may fear that our finances are getting out of control but if we tell ourselves to "stop worrying so much" we won't take steps to get our financial house in order. We may feel guilty that we have lied to our spouse, but if we tell ourselves "it's not that big of a deal" then we won't apologize and make amends so that we can regain a strong connection with her. If we feel shame and ignore the feeling we will not root out the irrational belief behind the shame and we will continue to feel less than loveable. When our hearts are consistently invalidated, we mistrust our emotions and do not act on them.

The final and fatal result of invalidation is, since we are really disconnected from our own hearts, we will not be able to connect our hearts with others and with God so we can feel the closeness and intimacy that God designed us to experience. All of the connection that we have with others will be a surface connection that does not feed the deep places of our soul.

Invalidation and Relationships

The first stage of relationship building is all about protecting and maintaining each person's value and power. Invalidation does just the opposite. When we invalidate someone we are letting them know that what they feel and what they love are not important. We are letting them know that they are only allowed to feel the feelings and love the things that are important to us.

Invalidation Exercise

Reread the list of examples of invalidating expressions:

Put a check mark next to the phrases you commonly heard growing up

Put an "x" next to the phrases that you commonly hear from people you are in relationship with today.

Underline the phrases that you commonly use with other people.

4 Why We Invalidate

If invalidating one another's emotions is so destructive, then why do we do it so often? There are several reasons why we might invalidate our own and others' emotions.

When things are going well in our connection with people and things we love, we feel pleasant emotions; when things are not, we feel painful emotions. Perhaps the simplest reason we invalidate our emotions is that we would rather feel pleasure than pain. We sometimes unwittingly invalidate other people's emotions because we want them to feel better. We think if we help them feel better we are being a good friend. In Chapter One we suggested a new goal when it comes to your feelings:

Instead of trying to feel good, try to feel deeply.

If you want to love well and connect deeply with others, here is a corollary to that goal:

Instead of trying to help others feel good, help others feel deeply.

By helping others feel deeply you are taking seriously how much they love whatever it is that the feeling is about. The first step in helping others feel deeply is to stop invalidating what they are feeling.

Sometimes we invalidate others' emotions as a way of avoiding our own emotions. When you feel sad I feel uncomfortable, so instead of allowing myself to feel uncomfortable (or even noticing that I feel uncomfortable) I tell you to cheer up. Or when you feel exposed I feel embarrassed, so I solve my problem by telling you it's not so bad.

We also invalidate *emotions* as a way of controlling people's *behavior*. We are afraid if we validate a child's anger then we are also validating their temper tantrum. We fear that if we validate someone's happiness in their achievement they will become arrogant and boastful, so we better take them down a notch right now ("don't be so full of yourself"). However, feeling something strongly and deeply doesn't necessarily lead to destructive behavior. And even when we sometimes choose to express our emotions in behaviors that are unhealthy, this doesn't mean the emotion itself is invalid or wrong.

Closely related to this is the concern that if we don't invalidate someone's emotions then we are also agreeing with whatever belief may be attached to that emotion. Let's say someone in your bible study group says "I'm so devastated. I don't know where to turn and I think God has abandoned me." In that moment, you have a decision whether allow them to feel their sadness and confusion, or to challenge their belief that God has abandoned them and quote Romans 8:28. You might even think that if you don't invalidate their emotion then you are not standing up for God and somehow agreeing with them that God has abandoned them. However, when we validate someone's emotions, we are not necessarily agreeing with them. We are simply affirming that it makes sense that someone who had that belief would feel those feelings.

If instead of validating the emotion we challenge their belief, what the speaker will experience is invalidation. What we are saying in essence is "If you were as smart (or spiritual, well-read, wise, or biblically knowledgeable) as me, you wouldn't feel that feeling. It is both arrogant and controlling to assert that we will only validate emotions if we agree with whatever belief they are connected to. Remember Job's friends? The first week they were with him they did a good job of empathizing with their friend, but after Job opened his mouth and began sharing the depth of what he was experiencing, they became his accusers because they were offended by the thoughts with which Job was struggling.

Far from validating someone's beliefs or behaviors, when we combine listening with empathy and validation we give people a great opportunity to examine their beliefs and behaviors. Often when we are feeling painful emotions the experience can be intense and overwhelming. When someone empathizes with us it gives us an opportunity to stand outside of ourselves and examine our thoughts and our behaviors and their relationship to what we feel. They help us to develop what psychologists call an *observing self,* which helps us to grow and become more defined. We develop the capacity to feel our feelings deeply and yet choose the behaviors that will help us. We develop the ability to feel our feelings deeply and also examine our belief system to see if there is anything we want to change.

Another reason we invalidate seems to me to be an epidemic in the church, and why the church is often so bad at loving well: it is the belief that if we feel anything other than happiness then we are letting God down, not living the Christian life correctly, and compromising our witness. Somehow we have bought into the idea that our emotional state is the greatest litmus test to whether or not we are close to God. And yet, according to Paul our goal is to "Rejoice with those who rejoice; mourn with those who mourn" (Romans 12:15), not tell people who are mourning that they should cheer up, pray more, and look on the positive side. Jesus himself experienced a range of painful feelings.[1] In Romans Paul states "I have great sorrow and unceasing anguish in my heart." The idea that Christians are not supposed to have painful feelings is foreign to the Bible.

Sometimes we invalidate others' emotions because we don't understand where they are coming from. We might be confused as to why they feel sad, or we might be confused as to why they feel sad to such an intense degree. I know someone who used to get intensely sad every year at Christmas. I couldn't understand this because, for me, Christmas is the best time of the year. It's a time to celebrate. It's a magical season. Yet year after year, the closer it got to December 25th, the sadder she would get. When I asked her about her sadness she didn't understand it either. Then one year, sometime in July, we were talking about her mother's death from cancer when she was a little girl. I asked when her mother died. You guessed it: Christmas Eve. Then her father remarried almost immediately and she was not allowed to grieve her mother's death – that would be considered a slap in the face to the new wife. So she buried the grief. But every year, as all the different Christmas traditions reminded her of that terrible time, the grief tried to resurface. Just because I didn't understand her sadness, it doesn't mean that her sadness didn't make sense.

This leads to two important axioms when it comes to learning how to use your heart to love well. Here's the first:

Your heart is smart.

Your heart knows when something important is going on even when your head has been trained to ignore it. Instead of ignoring it or invalidating it, learn to become curious about where your emotions and the emotions of others are coming from. Here is the second axiom:

If you don't understand where an emotion is coming from, it's because you don't understand where an emotion is coming from.

The problem is not with the emotion, the problem is with the understanding.

A Missed Opportunity

I was in a McDonald's playroom once with my young son and overheard a conversation with a child and her grandmother in which the grandmother missed a great opportunity to love well. The child was playing with two "My Little Ponies" and having lots of fun, then out of the blue looked at her grandmother with wide eyes and said, "I want to get the pink pony!" Now, here was a chance for the grandmother to connect with her granddaughter's heart. She could have said, "Wow, sounds like that would be fun for you to have the pink one." This would have encouraged the little girl to take her wants seriously and enjoy dreaming about the things she wants. It also probably would have led to more conversation about *why* she wanted the new pink pony, which would have given the grandmother more insight into her young heart. She might have said, "Yeah, pink is my favorite color," or "I like ponies, I want to ride ponies someday," or "My best friend has the pink pony and I want to get one so we can play with them together," or "If I get the pink pony I'll have all of them," or "In the cartoon the blue pony is always sad when the pink pony isn't around," or one of a hundred other surprising responses. Whatever the response, it would have been a key to understanding how this unique and precious heart was designed. The grandmother could have then validated her and said "it sure makes sense that you would be so excited about getting the pink pony!"

What did the grandmother choose to say? A very abrasive "You don't need the pink pony!" Translation: "I'm not interested in your excitement about what you want; don't want anything that you don't need; whatever it is about you that leads you to be excited about wanting this, shut it down." Why would the grandmother make this choice? Maybe she thought that being excited about wanting things leads to selfishness, so she needed to shut the girl's excitement down to control her character. Maybe she was uncomfortable with wanting things strongly herself. Maybe she thought that if she validated the child's wanting the pony then the little girl would ask her to buy the pony, and she couldn't afford to do that, which would make the little girl sad, and feeling sad is a bad thing and should be avoided at all costs!

But is it a bad thing? Let's play out what that potential conversation could have looked like:

Granddaughter: I want to get the pink pony!

Grandmother: Wow. You sound really excited about getting the pink pony!

Granddaughter: Yep. Did you know the pink one is a princess pony?

Grandmother: She is? You sure love princesses. It makes sense that you would want the pink pony!

Granddaughter: Yeah, I've wanted it for a long time.

Grandmother: Sounds like it's real important to you. I hope you can get it someday.

Granddaughter: Will you get it for me, grandma?

Grandmother: I can't get it right now, honey.

Granddaughter: (Beginning to cry) But I want it really bad.

Grandmother: Sounds like it's very sad for you not to get the

pony right now.
   Granddaughter: Yes I'm very sad. I want the pink pony.
   Grandmother: That sure makes sense. I get sad too when I want something really bad and I can't get it.

In this conversation the grandmother can stay connected to her granddaughter's heart and also help her practice feeling her feelings and understand what her feelings mean. This highlights another axiom when it comes to using your heart:

You can either help people excavate their hearts, or help them bury their hearts.

I'm sure the grandmother at McDonalds didn't have any evil intentions towards her granddaughter. I'm guessing she wasn't giving too much thought about the way she was communicating and how it might impact the young girl. But the reality is she was telling her granddaughter to bury her heart – to shut it down one little step at a time. But what would it be like going into each conversation knowing that you have an opportunity to help someone excavate her heart – to understand more fully what is important to her? To help her understand what her feelings mean about the people and things she loves? In the next chapter we will begin learning how to have these kinds of conversations throughout the day with our spouses, children, friends and co-workers, so that we can help them live with their hearts fully alive and stay connected with them.

Personal Reflection

In which relationship are your feelings invalidated most often? How does that impact your relationship?

In which relationship do you invalidate the other person's

feelings most often? How does that impact your relationship?

5 Paying Attention to Feelings

In the last two chapters we have talked about the importance of our emotions. We have stated that the most important thing you need to understand about your emotions is this:

Your emotions are signals that let you know the current state of connection with the people and things you love.

Here is the corollary:

Other people's emotions are signals that let you know the current state of connection with the people and things they love.

Therefore, if you want to connect with people in a significant way, one critical thing you must do is to understand what they are feeling. Here is the bottom line: if you don't care about what people are feeling, then you don't care about what they love. It's that simple. On the other hand, if you care about what people love, then the best way to stay connected with them is understand what is going on in their emotional world.

Remember that the critical thing in Stage One of relationship building is maintaining the value and power of each person. Whenever we help people bury their hearts, we make them less powerful and treat them with less value. Whenever we help people excavate their hearts we empower them to be who they really are, and we treat who they are as valuable, as worth paying attention to.

So, the first skill you need to learn in order to listen to people's hearts is to pay attention to what they are feeling, so that you know what is happening in their relationships with the people and things they love. You will be able to understand if things are going well with the people they love, or if something is being threatened, or if something is lost or missing. You will be aware if they feel they have damaged a relationship, or if they have drifted into a place where they feel unlovable. These are all priceless things to know if you want to love someone well.

Take a moment and think about the people closest to you and what they are experiencing today. What does your spouse or girlfriend feel about her job? What does she feel about herself as a parent? What does she feel about her relationship with God? What does she feel about her significance? What does she feel about her home? What does she feel about her hobbies and interests? What does she feel about her parents? And of all these different feelings, which are really intense today, and which are more subdued?

If you are a parent, think about one of your children: What does he feel about his best friend? What does he feel about school? What does he feel about the way he looks? What does he feel about his hobbies? What does he feel about his own importance? What does he feel about his brothers or sisters? And of all these, which feelings are almost overwhelming to him and which ones are more mild? Ask yourself the same sorts of questions about the other people in your life: your parents, your siblings, your friends, your colleagues.

Or you can start from the other end. Think about your spouse or boyfriend: Where is he feeling happy these days? Where is he feeling sad? In what relationship is he feeling angry or afraid? Where is he feeling confused? Where is he feeling guilty or ashamed or lonely? And, again, which of these feelings are always on the front burner and which are less intense and in the background? Then ask yourself the same questions about all the people who are important to you.

The more you know the answers to these questions, the more deeply connected you will be with the people in your life. Unfortunately, as we have seen in the last two chapters, we have become adept at ignoring, minimizing and even belittling the emotions of the people around us.

Over the next few chapters we are going to be practicing several basic skills that will help you listen to the hearts of the people you want to love well. And not surprisingly, it begins with simply being able to identify what people are feeling at any given moment. When you have practiced being aware of what people are feeling, then you will always be aware of things that they love – the things that are most important to them.

Two ways to tune in

There are two ways to tune into what people are feeling. The first way to identify what others are feeling is to simply notice what feeling words they use while they are speaking:

> *I'm really ticked off...*
> *That scares me to death...*
> *I'm feeling sad about...*

As you practice breaking the habit of invalidating people's emotions, you may be surprised at how often people use these feeling words and what a great insight they give you into what matters most to them.

The second way to tune into what people are feeling is to pay attention to what is being communicated non-verbally, either through tone of voice or through body language. Research has shown that over 90 percent of communication is non-verbal. Body language, facial expressions and tone of voice can all be strong indications of what someone is feeling. Therefore it is important to not only pay attention to what people say, but also to how they say it.

As you tune into what people are feeling, through either verbal or non-verbal communication, practice remembering what that feeling means. If someone says "I'm really ticked off..." practice remembering that anger means that something they love is being threatened. If someone says "I'm feeling sad about..." practice remembering that this means they have lost something that they loved.

As you practice this simple skill, you will be amazed at how much more connected you will be with the people in your life

Practice exercise: Identify what people are feeling

In the following sentences, try to identify what the speaker might be feeling. It doesn't matter if you are wrong or right (we will talk more about that later), just that you attempt to understand and name the emotion.

1. _discouragement_   *Your friend makes no eye contact and with a lifeless voice says "God doesn't seem to be answering my prayers at all."*

2. _shame_   *Your spouse says "I'm so furious with myself! I can't believe I bounced a check!"*

3. _forgotten / lonely_   *Your sister says "I wish John would call. I really miss him."*

4. _Encouraged / loved_   *A friend gives a beaming smile and says "I got the greatest compliment from my dad today!"*

5. _Frustrated / unappreciated_   *A co-worker shakes her head and in a sarcastic tone of voice says "I love my job. I'm so glad I went to college for four years."*

6. _disappointment_   *Your daughter says "This is the worst summer I have ever had!"*

7. _Guilt, Embarrassment_   *An employee you supervise says "I need to apologize to Larry. I took way too long to get him his numbers and then he had to work overtime to get his report done."*

8. _Overwhelmed, discouraged_   *You ask a friend if they have had a good week and they roll their eyes, shake their head, and say nothing.*

9. _Fear / Anxiety_   *A spouse says "My boss is going to kill me when he gets back from his conference!"*

10. *Regret/fear* Your son says "I think I really hurt Tammy's feelings. I wish I could just keep my mouth closed sometimes."

11. *Shame* A friend at church says "I wonder if God is disappointed with me. It seems like I'm always letting him down."

12. *Happy* Your boss pumps her fist and says "Two more weeks and I'm on the beach in Hawaii!"

13. *Disappointed* Your best friend says "I got out my shorts for this summer and not a single pair from last year fits. I feel like such a loser."

14. *Confusion* A friend says "We might have found a house. We really like the school system but it's quite a bit further from work and church. It's also a little bit more than we wanted to pay."

15. *Fear* A friend says "We have a meeting at work tomorrow about potential downsizing. It's really stressing me out."

Practice exercise: Listening to the heart

For the next 24 hours, pay attention to what the people you are relating to are feeling. Listen for feeling words and also pay attention to their body language, facial expressions, and tone of voice. Try to name the emotion in your own mind.

Personal reflection:

How difficult or easy was it for you to pay attention to people's emotions for the past 24 hours?

Which emotion is the hardest for you to allow others to feel?
Why do you think that is?

6 Listening to the Heart

When others are talking about the people and things they love, there are usually two parts to the communication: a feeling and a thought. When we pay attention to the feeling we learn what is happening in a relationship with something that is loved, when we pay attention to the thought we learn specifically what relationship is being impacted and what specifically happened to cause the impact. If I smile and say "My boss told me today that he wants me to enter the management training program at work!" there are two parts to my communication:

1. A feeling = happiness, excitement, pride = there is a strong connection with a love relationship
2. A thought = the boss wants to prepare me for a major promotion = the specific relationship is with myself as a professional or as a provider for my family.

In order to fully listen to the people that we love, we need to pay attention to both the feelings and the thoughts that are being expressed to get the full picture of what is happening in their hearts.

You may be wondering: what if I disagree with the thought? What if someone says "I'm so worried that John will leave me for someone else" and we think that there is no way that is ever going to happen? Wouldn't it be more helpful to point out all the reasons John isn't going to leave? We will deal with this question more fully when we talk about respect, but the short answer here is no, it is not helpful at all. And here is why. What you are really saying when you take this approach is "If you were as smart as I am you wouldn't be feeling what you are feeling." This approach will always come across as judgmental, belittling or arrogant. It is just another form of invalidating.

Sometimes when you learn new habits, you have to unlearn old, bad habits at the same time. If you have a habit of listening to others primarily to judge, evaluate, critique or debate their thoughts, then this is a place where you will have to unlearn some bad habits. I'm not saying that there is never a time to challenge someone's thoughts; I'm just saying this is not the place (hint: the time to challenge someone's thoughts will come later when they trust our perspective and our love for them enough that they *invite us* to challenge them).

Remember, we are working on how to lay a foundation for a healthy relationship, so we are focusing on *understanding* the person.

I have found that a helpful process for me in this instance is to ask myself "When have I felt this angry? Or sad? Or embarrassed?" This takes my focus off of trying to evaluate why people are feeling what they feel, and changes it to trying to understand them. If your friend is worried about losing his job, you might be tempted to evaluate the chances that this might happen and invalidate the feeling. If instead you ask yourself "When was the last time I was this worried about something?" and you remember the time you were waiting to hear test results from your doctor. You remember the gnawing in the pit of your stomach. Now you are in a position to identify with your friend as you listen to his heart. You might be surprised at how much more connected you feel to the people in your life just by taking a moment to identify with what they are feeling before responding to them.

This can be especially helpful when listening to children, whose emotional responses may seem overblown. If your child is distraught because she's sick and can't go to a birthday party, it might be tempting to tell her "it's just a party, don't make such a big deal out of it." If instead you take a moment and remember how disappointing it was to have to miss the football game you had tickets for because your car broke down, you will be in a position to understand her sadness and empathize with her.

Reflecting back the thought and feeling

Now we are going to use what we practiced in the last chapter to learn how to reflect back to someone what they have said in a way that they feel understood and valued. This is sometimes referred to as reflective listening or listening with empathy and it involves three things:

1. Identifying the feeling
2. Identifying the thought
3. Reflecting both the feeling and thought back to the speaker in a tentative statement. For example:

I'm so tired of these confusing emails that I get from my boss!

Feeling = frustration

Thought = the boss's confusing communication

Reflecting thought and feeling in a tentative statement = *It sounds like you are frustrated about the way your boss communicates.*

The main reason you want to be tentative when you reflect back is that you may have misunderstood the speaker. And since it is your goal to connect with the heart of the speaker, you want to make sure to give them an opportunity to let you know when you are not on target. There are several important ways this might be the case:

Wrong emotion: you may have identified the wrong emotion. You might have heard fear when someone was expressing anger.

Too intense: you might have identified outrage when the speaker was trying to communicate frustration.

Too mild: you might have identified disappointment when the speaker was trying to communicate feeling crushed.

Wrong thought: You might have heard that someone is angry at their boss for not recognizing their performance, when they were trying to say that they were angry with themselves for not performing to their own expectations.

In fact, as you practice reflective listening, you may be surprised by two things. First, you may be surprised at how often you are wrong in one of these four areas. We tend to go through life assuming we have understood everyone on the first attempt until we start reflecting back what they have said only to find out how often we are a bit off! Secondly, you may be surprised at how little it matters if you are wrong as long as you are tentative in your reflective listening. The speaker will very rarely get upset. Why is this so? Think about what you have just done. In essence, you have said to the speaker: "I really care about what is happening in your heart. I think you are saying this is *what is happening* in your heart, and I think you are saying this is *why it is happening*. Am I right?"

Now think about your own life. How many times have you come home at the end of the day and thought "I'm so sick and tired of everybody trying to understand me! All day long people are paying attention to what matters to me and I'm fed up!"? You have probably never thought that. Neither have the people you know. So, don't worry if you are inaccurate in your listening, because they will sense that you are at least trying to understand. They will simply rephrase what they have said to help you zero in closer. Then you can repeat the listening process until they let you know that you have understood them.

Speaker: I start my new assignment at work tomorrow. It's the biggest project I've ever supervised. I don't know if I will get much sleep tonight.

You: Am I hearing you say you are nervous about taking on such a big responsibility.

Speaker: No way. I'm thrilled. I can't stop thinking about all the different ways to attack this project.

You: O.K. Sounds like you are really charged up and can't wait to get going!

Speaker: Exactly. I can't wait until tomorrow. I haven't been this excited about going to work in over a year.

Another reason to be tentative when you reflect is that, even when you have correctly identified the speaker's thoughts and feelings, a tentative question invites the speaker to continue sharing more about their heart if they so desire.

Speaker: I start my new assignment at work tomorrow. It's the biggest project I've ever supervised. I don't know if I will get much sleep tonight.

You: Wow! Sounds like you are really excited and can't wait to get going!

Speaker: Exactly. I can't wait until tomorrow. I haven't been this excited about going to work in over a year.

You: Sounds like getting a big challenge to conquer has rekindled your passion at work.

Speaker: It sure has. You know, for a few months I was thinking about finding a new job. I was so bored. I think I'm realizing that I really need a challenge to be motivated.

You: I think I'm hearing that you're kind of surprised by this discovery that you need to challenge to stay engaged. Is that right?

Speaker: I think it is. You know, I've had a big problem staying consistent with my exercising. I wonder if a big challenge would get me going again in that area, too.

There are a lot of phrases that you can use to make sure your reflection is tentative:

It sounds like...

Am I hearing you say...
I think I'm hearing...
Are you saying...
If I'm hearing you right...

Sometimes when people are learning to listen reflectively it might feel a little wooden or canned to use these kind of tentative statements. It might not feel natural at first. If that is what you feel, you are not alone. That is a common experience in learning most new skills. If you pick up a guitar for the first time and try to play what comes naturally, what you will get is a lot of noise. You have to learn how to play a chord, which entails holding your hand in a way that feels very unnatural and awkward. Then you have to learn more chords, all of which feel just as awkward as the first. The key is to keep practicing until what at first felt unnatural feels like the only way you would ever do it.

Think about young kids learning how to swing a baseball bat. Usually they want to keep their arms straight while swinging. It doesn't feel natural to bend their arms and swing with their wrists, but with enough practice it not only feels natural it becomes unconscious behavior – they do it without even thinking about it. Then years later if those same kids begin to learn how to golf, what happens? They want to swing the club like a baseball bat. Why? Because through lots of repetition it just feels natural. The same experience is true with all of the skills we will practice in learning how to use our hearts to love well. Don't make the mistake of believing that feeling natural and being genuine are the same thing. Feeling natural only means you have practiced the behavior to the point that you no longer have to think about it (whether the behavior is harmful or helpful). Being genuine means you really want to connect with someone (whether it feels natural yet or not).

Red Flag: Some people use words to communicate and to understand; others use words to control and manipulate. Sometimes you will find that there are people who do not want you to use reflective listening skills when you are speaking with them. Even if you explain that you are just trying to make sure you understand what they are saying they will still resist. I have heard people say things like "stop using techniques" or "stop trying to handle me." Even when I ask if there is a better way that I could make sure that I am tracking with what they are thinking and feeling there is strong resistance. When this happens it is usually because the person speaking is not using their words to communicate but to be in control and make sure they get their way. They really don't want communication to be clear, because the more fog they can create the more they are likely to get what they want. This is a huge red flag to look for when choosing people to be in relationship with: Are they using words to communicate or are they using words to manipulate? There is absolutely no way you can have a relationship where each person has equal value and power with someone who uses words to stay in control.

Practice exercise: Reflective listening

Let's look again at the sentences we used in the last chapter. This time identify the feeling, the thought, and then write a reflective listening sentence that begins with a tentative statement, and includes both the feeling and the thought of the speaker. Try to use a variety of tentative statements. As before, it doesn't matter if you get the emotion and the thought exactly correct. What matters is you make an attempt to understand.

Example: *The house seems so empty since Candice went to college.*

Emotion = Lonely
Thought = Candice is no longer at home
Reflecting thought and feeling in a tentative statement = *It sounds like you have been lonely since Candice left home.*

1. *Your friend makes no eye contact and with a lifeless voice says "God doesn't seem to be answering my prayers at all."*
Emotion = discouragement
Thought = she feels like she's in a helpless situation

Reflecting thought and feeling in a tentative statement =
Sounds like your really wrestling with something

2. *Your spouse says "I'm so furious with myself! I can't believe I bounced a check!*

Emotion = *Shame/Anger*
Thought = *She hates making mistakes*
Reflecting thought and feeling in a tentative statement =

Sounds like your worried about making mistake
Are you   frustrated

3. *Your sister says "I wish John would call. I really miss him."*

Emotion = *loneliness, abandon, sadness*
Thought = *I feel disconnected and I really don't went to*
Reflecting thought and feeling in a tentative statement =

Sounds like your lonely and would love to connect

4. *A friend gives a beaming smile and says "I got the greatest compliment from my dad today!"*

Emotion = *happiness encouraged*
Thought = *That feels like an unexpected they*
Reflecting thought and feeling in a tentative statement =
Sounds like your envoy

5. *A co-worker shakes her head and in a sarcastic tone of voice says "I love my job. I'm so glad I went to college for four years."*

Emotion = *minimized / unappreciated*
Thought = *I'm better worthy more than this*
Reflecting thought and feeling in a tentative statement =
and It hard to feel appreciated when
Having o hard day   Do you feel

6. *Your daughter says "This is the worst summer I have ever had!"*

Emotion = *Frustration*
Thought = *She's unhappy*
Reflecting thought and feeling in a tentative statement =
Why do you say that, you
I hate to hear that
I can tell your unhappy
whats going on

7. *An employee you supervise says "I need to apologize to Larry.*
I took way too long to get him his numbers and then he had to
work overtime to get his report done."

Emotion =
Thought = *Seems like*
yourself conscience
with how give people
Reflecting thought and feeling in a tentative statement = *What they*
Are you disappointed with/ Seems like you need
Do you / may have let 2
Larry down ?

8. *You ask a friend if they have had a good week and they roll*
their eyes, shake their head, and say nothing.

Emotion =
Thought =
Reflecting thought and feeling in a tentative statement =

9. *Your spouse says "My boss is going to kill me when he gets*
back from his conference!"

Emotion =
Thought =
Reflecting thought and feeling in a tentative statement =

10. *Your son says "I think I really hurt Tammy's feelings. I wish*
I could just keep my mouth closed sometimes."

Emotion =
Thought =
Reflecting thought and feeling in a tentative statement =

11. *A friend at church says "I wonder if God is disappointed with me. I seems like I'm always letting him down."*
    Emotion =
    Thought =
    Reflecting thought and feeling in a tentative statement =

12. *Your boss pumps her fist and says "Two more weeks and I'm on the beach in Hawaii!"*
    Emotion =
    Thought =
    Reflecting thought and feeling in a tentative statement =

13. *Your best friend says "I got out my shorts for this summer and not a single pair from last year fits. I feel like such a loser."*
    Emotion =
    Thought =
    Reflecting thought and feeling in a tentative statement =

14. *A friend says "We might have found a house. We really like the school system but it's quite a bit further from work and church. It's also a little bit more than we wanted to pay."*
    Emotion =
    Thought =
    Reflecting thought and feeling in a tentative statement =

15. *A friend says "We have a meeting at work tomorrow about potential downsizing. It's really stressing me out."*
    Emotion =

Thought =
Reflecting thought and feeling in a tentative statement =

Practice exercise: Reflective listening

Get a practice partner. Each day spend five minutes reflective listening to what is going on in their lives, and then let them spend five minutes reflective listening to what is going on in your life.

Practice exercise: Reflective Listening

Think about a time you are going to be meeting with someone over the next couple of days. It might be with your family at dinner or it might be meeting a friend for coffee. Plan on taking five minutes of that meeting and, without letting them know what you are doing, practice reflective listening. Try to do this exercise three times over the next week.

7 Validating the Heart

Validation is an important tool to have in your relational tool belt if you want to help people excavate their heart. As the name suggests, it is the opposite of invalidation: instead of telling people their feelings make no sense, you affirm the appropriateness of their feelings.

How to Validate

Validating someone's emotions is as simple as agreeing that you can understand how they would feel what they are feeling:

It sure makes sense that you would be devastated by that news.
I can see why you are feeling so hurt by your mom's letter.
If I were in your shoes I would be feeling the same way.

If we have been in a situation that is very similar to what the speaker is going through and felt the same way we can use our shared experience as a powerful way to validate their emotion:

It sure makes sense to me that you would be so confused and angry. I was laid off two years ago and felt the same things.

Sometimes the best way to validate someone's emotion is to acknowledge that you have *not* experienced what they are going through and that you have no point of comparison for the intensity of their emotion:

I can't imagine how painful it must be to go through that.

Sometimes we have a difficult time validating other's emotions, because we simply disagree with the person's perception of the world. When this happens it is challenging for us to not think their emotions are wrong somehow. This brings up a critical point for us to understand:

Emotions always say something true: sometimes they say something true about the outside world, and sometimes they say something true about our inner world.

If a man feels angry or frightened because his wife is joking around with another man, it might say something true about the outside world (his wife may be doing something inappropriate), or it might say something about his inner world (maybe he has some unhealed wounding from a previous relationship where someone cheated on him).

If a woman feels angry or frightened because her boss criticized her work, it might say something about the outside world (her boss may have given the criticism in a rude or threatening manner) or it might say something about her inside world (maybe whenever her mother criticized her she also withdrew all support and affection for a season).

The trap we often fall into is invalidating people's emotions because we don't believe they say anything real about the outside world:

Don't be ridiculous John! There's nothing wrong with a little joking around!

Stop overreacting! So your boss criticized your report, big deal!

When we do this we are not connecting with others' hearts, we are evaluating their hearts. We can also lose a great opportunity because we not only help people bury their hearts in this moment, we prevent them from excavating their hearts and discovering something that might need to be healed. We need to slow down in our rush to judge, evaluate, and fix others, and instead take the time needed to allow them to explore what is going on inside of them.

This is exactly what James, one of the leaders of the early church, says in his letter:

My dear brothers and sisters, take note of this: Everyone should be quick to listen, slow to speak and slow to become angry. (James 1:19)

We can do this by simply connecting people's emotions to the thoughts that they have expressed:

It sounds like you're upset because you believe your wife was acting seductively with another man. If I believed that, I would be upset as well.
It sounds like you're scared because you believe your boss threatened to demote you over a simple mistake. If I thought that, I would be nervous, too.

Notice in the above instances that speaker is not agreeing with the belief of the person they are validating, they are merely saying if they shared that belief then they would feel the same way.
We can affirm the appropriateness of the emotion even when we don't understand the cause of the emotion or its intensity, or when the speaker doesn't understand the cause of the emotion or its intensity. Sometimes we just can't connect the dots. Sometimes when this happens it is because the speaker has some emotional baggage of which they are unaware. For example, post-traumatic stress can make a very harmless situation seem very frightening. If we invalidate the feeling we rob the speaker of the opportunity to explore and heal their own heart. Or perhaps someone has a chemical imbalance that is creating a painful emotional reaction. If we minimize the emotions we can deter someone from getting the medical help they need. In such situations we can still affirm the appropriateness of the emotion even when neither we nor the speaker understand where it's coming from:

Your heart is smart. I'm sure there's a good reason you feel that.

When to Validate

There are times when validation can be especially helpful. The first is when you hear people invalidate or minimize the emotions they are trying to express. Because invalidation is such a common practice, people often have a hard time accepting their own emotions. Often you will hear people invalidate their own feelings with phrases like:

> *I know I shouldn't get angry, but...*
> *I shouldn't be afraid...*
> *I should feel thankful, but I'm really sad...*

Sometimes you hear people minimize their feelings with statements like:

> *I know I have no right to get so angry...* (Translation: It's okay to be a little bit angry, but the intensity of anger I'm feeling is wrong).

When the people you want to love well say things like this it's a signal that they are not taking their own hearts seriously. Somewhere along the line they have been taught to bury their hearts. By validating their feelings you give them permission to own and explore what their feelings are trying to teach them.

Another time when it is helpful to validate is when someone has expressed a particularly intense emotion, or an emotion that society generally considers a "bad" or "weak" emotion. Often the speaker can feel exposed and uncomfortable after expressing such an emotion, and validation helps to normalize their experience. Also validation in these moments lets people know they are not alone. To know that someone understands and accepts them can ease the isolation that painful feelings sometimes brings. I remember a time when a woman told me about a tragic experience her sister was going through, and how angry her sister was at God. Then she asked me what she should tell her sister. I know she was wondering what she could tell her sister so that she would stop feeling angry at God, but that's not what I told her. Instead I told her she could say "it sure makes sense that you are so angry at God. If I was going through what you are going through I would feel angry too." God has big shoulders. He can tolerate people being angry with him. He knows it means that something they love is being threatened and they are trying to protect it. God never goes away when we are angry, he always draws near. If this woman could validate her sister in this moment it would help her sister to not feel judged or crazy or alone, and she could stay connected to her sister's heart as she worked through her pain.

The value of validating other's intense emotions is just as important when listening to children and teens. Even though it seems that the things that make children sad, angry or scared are minor concerns in the grand scheme of life, remember that they are just learning how to use their hearts. For children, just as for adults, each emotion is a signal about something that is happening in a relationship with people and things they love. When you validate their intense feelings you help them to not bury their hearts and give them a foundation for loving well.

As children enter their teen years and begin bringing their heart into the adult world emotions intensify even more. Sometimes adults can look back on their teenage years with a sense of nostalgia, and even things like the first love or the first break-up can be remembered with a bit of humor. This can cloud our ability to empathize and validate with teens when they are going through what is the most exhilarating or most painful experiences they have ever had. We can unintentionally belittle what they feel instead of helping them embrace their feelings as part of learning how to love fully. I think one of the biggest disconnects between teens and their parents is a lack of empathy and validation. On some level teens are aware that this invalidation is actually an inability to see and value who they are as individuals.

One final word about when to validate: because validation is so important, always make sure you understand what someone is feeling before you validate that feeling. It can be frustrating and confusing for someone when we validate their sadness when they were trying to communicate anger or fear. It's a good rule of thumb to practice reflective listening first before validating.

Practice Exercise: Validating the Heart

Go back and read the reflective listening sentences that you wrote in chapter 7. Assume that the speaker responds that you understand what they were saying, and for each one write a validating sentence here. Try to find a variety of ways to express validation.

1.

2.

3.

4.

5.

6.

7.

8.

9.

10.

11.

12.

13.

14.

15.

8 Two Helpful Sentences

As you practice empathizing and validating others, you will discover that they are willing to share more of what is going on in the deep places of their hearts with you. This will help you build a stronger relationship, but will also create some challenges that, depending on how you respond, will either shut down communication or encourage more sharing. Fortunately, these challenges can be overcome by learning two simple but critical sentences.

Sentence #1: "Thanks for sharing that with me."

When someone has shared something significant with you, they have paid you a huge compliment by trusting you with the deeper places of their heart. They have also given you a great gift, the chance to see what is really going on inside them. It is important when this happens to express value for the compliment and the gift by thanking them. When you thank them for sharing you let them know that you do not take this gift for granted, and that it is important to you to continue to get to know them on a heart-to-heart level.

There is another important reason to thank someone for sharing their heart. Sometimes when someone has shared on a deeper level than they have before with you, there can be an awkward moment even after they have been empathized with and validated. There are a couple reasons for this.

The first reason for the awkward moment has to do with the nature of self-disclosure. Self-disclosure is complicated by two contrasting needs: the desire to be accepted, and the desire to be known. The risk of self-disclosure is that if we disclose parts of ourselves that might be different from others then we may not be accepted. The risk of not disclosing is that we will have a sense that the others don't know who we really are, and therefore any acceptance we get feels shallow and unfulfilling.

Because of this, when someone has risked self-disclosure,

they might have created a "risk gap" in the relationship. They might wonder: Am I still accepted after I've shared something that might be a little different? Are you thinking I'm weak or unspiritual or selfish or shallow? Was it a mistake to let you know this about me?

The second problem with self-disclosure is that self-disclosure equals commitment. We always have the option to disclose parts of ourselves or to keep them private. By choosing to disclose a part of herself, your friend is actually making a small, personal investment in the relationship. She is deciding that this relationship is important enough to go a little bit deeper. The more a person chooses to self-disclose, the more there is at stake in the friendship. In a sense, when someone lets you know what is going on in the deep places of their heart it's almost as if they said something like "I like you" or "You are important to me" or "I want to be closer friends with you." Usually when someone says these kinds of statements directly or overtly, the other person reciprocates ("You are important to me, too").

Therefore, the speaker might have also created an "intimacy gap" in the relationship: I have just said that you are very important to me, am I important to you as well? Do you value how hard it was for me to share this with you?

While we might not be aware of the reason for the awkwardness of being in these gaps, we feel the weight of them. We feel something more needs to be said or done.

Fortunately, closing the "intimacy gap" and the "risk gap" is as simple as thanking your friend for sharing his heart with you:

Phil, thanks for sharing that struggle with me.
Barb, I really appreciate your willingness to share that experience with me.
Sweetheart, it sure means a lot to me that you would share that pain with me. Thanks.

By thanking the person for his self-disclosure, you close the intimacy gap by letting him know that his sharing is deeply valued, and you close the risk gap by communicating that they are accepted for who they really are, struggles and all.

Sentence #2: *"Is there any way I can be helpful?"*

Besides the two gaps we just mentioned, there is another reason we sometimes feel awkward when someone is talking about the deep places of their heart. Often when someone shares an intense emotion they are talking about a personal problem with which they are struggling. It might be a practical problem, an old wound, a developmental issue, an emotional struggle, a doubt, or any number of other concerns. Further, when someone shares a struggle like this there is usually some pain attached to it.

As human beings we are not comfortable with either problems or pain. When someone expresses either a problem or pain we feel that something should be done to either solve the problem or take away the pain.

Often when someone expresses pain we feel a responsibility to make them feel better. We try to cheer them up by telling them it's not really that bad, or that other people have it much worse off, or that they should look on the positive side. As well-intended as these suggestions are, they all result in invalidating the speaker's emotion.

Another common response is to feel some responsibility to fix their problem for them, or at least give them advice on how to fix their problem. We think if we can fix people's problems then we will take away their pain. Sometimes we want to tell them a book to read that will solve their problem, or tell them what we would do if we had that problem, or give them a scripture verse that solves their problem, or tell them that if they pray more God will take the problem away, or tell them a habit to develop, or one of a hundred other simple solutions. The reality, however, is that our problems are rarely simple. They are often a complex web of issues that may take us a while to untangle. If they were as simple as praying a prayer, we would have solved them ourselves years ago.

We think we are helping when we try to solve people's problems for them, but in reality we are devaluing the depth and the complexity of the struggle. In a sense we are saying, "This thing you have struggled with the past 10 years is not that big of a deal. If you were as smart (or wise, spiritual, well-read, disciplined, etc.) as me you wouldn't have this problem. After all, I have given you the solution in just three minutes!"

Along with giving the impression that their problem is a simple problem to solve, we can also unintentionally communicate that the person is weak, unintelligent, unspiritual, lazy, or a host of other defects of character or competence. After all, if the problem will be solved by the simple suggestion we have just given, then the question arises "why haven't you solved this already?"

Another big concern in solving others' problems is we have not been given permission to solve their problems. The speaker has been brave enough to take the risk of sharing something personal and vulnerable, and perhaps all they want at this point is to be understood and known, to not be alone in the midst of their struggle. They have not yet asked for our help and they may not want our help. We may not have earned their trust in either our character or our capacity in helping them solve their problem. The reality is that sharing about a struggle we are having is one level of intimacy, while inviting others to help us solve our problems is a deeper level of intimacy involving more trust and vulnerability. It's great when people invite us into a deeper level of intimacy with their hearts, but it is never a good idea to push our way in.

And yet, when someone is in pain, or when they are struggling with an immense burden, simply listening, validating, and thanking them for sharing doesn't always seem to be enough. Aren't we supposed to help each other? If we don't offer some kind of practical help isn't that a signal that we don't care? It can feel heartless to see someone wrestle with these kind of concerns and *not* help them.

Fortunately, there is a simple way to address this concern. If you are wondering if the person would like your help, ask them:

Is there any way I can be a support to you?
Is there any way I can be helpful?
Is there anything you need from me as you face this struggle?

Is there anything you want from me that would be helpful?

First, by asking the question in this way you communicate that, while you are willing to help, you understand it is their problem, not yours, and that they are strong enough and smart enough to figure out what help they need and who they need it from.

Secondly, by asking these kinds of questions your friend stays in control of her level of self-disclosure. She is given the choice to decide whether or not she is ready to ask for help, and what specific kind of help to ask for. For some people the mere act of asking for help is an extremely vulnerable experience. It is better to ask *"Is there any way I can help you with this?"* than to ask *"What help do you need from me?"* because the second question assumes that speaker needs and wants help from you.

Thus, by asking this simple question you have *supported* the speaker's heart by letting her know that you are on her side and that you are willing to help, and you have *empowered* her heart by communicating that you understand that she is a strong, competent adult who can handle her own problems.

Personal Reflection:

How difficult is it for you to allow people to talk about their pain and problems and believe that they are smart enough and strong enough to solve their problems without your advice?

Part Two:

Loving Well by Protecting Others' Value

9 Warmth

*Love one another with genuine affection, and take delight in
honoring each other.*
Romans 12:10 (NLT)

Imagine a mom coming home after a long day's work and as soon as she opens the front door her two year old yells "Mommy!" and runs smiling to give the mother a big hug. That's warmth.

Imagine walking into a restaurant where you are a regular customer, where you have taken the time to get to know the staff, and where you have always tipped *very* well. What kind of greeting do you think you will get? I'm guessing the staff will smile when you come in, call you by name, and say something like "It's so great to see you!" That's also warmth.

Imagine being at work and another employee comes in and doesn't make eye contact with anyone, doesn't smile or say "hi", and goes about his business frowning and huffing and puffing. That's an absence of warmth.

When we experience warmth from others we feel valued. Sometimes we valued just for who we are (as the two-year-old values her mother), and sometimes we feel valued for what we do (for example, because we are big tippers). When we interact with someone and we don't experience warmth we feel devalued. In this chapter we are going to be focusing on the first kind of warmth, where we express value to people just for who they are.

The Source of Value

There are three things that I believe are true about every single person that you meet. First, every person you meet is made in the image of God. The writer of Genesis tells us:

Then God said, "Let us make mankind in our image, in our likeness, so that they may rule over the fish in the sea and the birds in the sky, over the livestock and all the wild animals, and over all the creatures that move along the ground." So God created mankind in his own image, in the image of God he created them; male and female he created them. (Genesis 1:26-27)

The second thing that is true about everyone you meet is that God loves that person so much that he sent his only son to die for that person. In one of the most well-known passages of the Bible Jesus states:

For God so loved the world that he gave his one and only Son, that whoever believes in him shall not perish but have eternal life. ¹⁷ For God did not send his Son into the world to condemn the world, but to save the world through him. (John 3:16-17)

The apostle Paul echoes this when he says that:

But God demonstrates His own love toward us, in that while we were yet sinners, Christ died for us. (Romans 5:8)

A third truth about everyone you meet is they have an eternal destiny. C.S. Lewis states this as well as it can be stated in one of the most compelling quotes I have ever read:

"It is a serious thing to live in a society of possible gods and goddesses, to remember that the dullest most uninteresting person you talk to may one day be a creature which, if you saw it now, you would be strongly tempted to worship, or else a horror and a corruption such as you now meet, if at all, only in a nightmare. All day long we are, in some degree helping each other to one or the other of these destinations. It is in the light of these overwhelming possibilities, it is with the awe and the circumspection proper to them, that we should conduct all of our dealings with one another, all friendships, all loves, all play, all politics. There are no ordinary people. You have never talked to a mere mortal. Nations, cultures, arts, civilizations - These are mortal, and their life is to ours as the life of a gnat. But it is immortals whom we joke with, work with, marry, snub, and exploit - immortal horrors or everlasting splendors."

C.S. Lewis, The Weight of Glory[1]

Every person you interact with bears the image of God, is so valuable that God sent his son to die on the cross for them, and has an eternal destiny that is either too wonderful or too horrible to be imagined. These three truths trump every other truth that could be said about each person you meet. These three truths are the source of value for each person you interact with. And it is why everyone you meet deserves to be treated with warmth. It is also why you deserve to be treated with warmth by each person you are in relationship with.

Sometimes we can focus on things that are less important: how others dress, how they talk, the choices they have made, what they believe, their addictive behaviors, or the level of success they have achieved. When we focus on these lesser things we can sometimes feel justified in not treating others as though they don't matter. And yet, in God's eyes the value is there whether we pay attention to or not.

Imagine for a moment you are an art expert and you've come across a painting in someone's attic that you immediately recognize as a lost Rembrandt. It might be dirty and torn and forgotten, but it is obviously the work of a master artist. Here's the question: when would you start treating that painting as though it were valuable? After the tear is repaired? After the dirt has been cleaned away? After other people also recognize that it is a lost Rembrandt? Probably not. You would probably immediately get it insured for millions and begin looking for the best art restorer you could find.

Every person you meet is one of God's lost masterpieces, and because of that each person deserves to be valued. Warmth is the way we express that value.

More Than Words

Warmth is not expressed primarily in words, but in our body language, facial expressions, and tone of voice. You can hear warmth in someone's tone of voice. You can see warmth in their smile and in their eyes. You can tell before they even say a word if they are glad to see you or not. Imagine you have an interaction with two different people, each of whom says "Hi, how's it going?" The first person speaks in a monotone voice while not making eye contact; the second person smiles, makes eye contact, and you can hear in their tone of voice that they are glad to see you. The words are the same, but the non-verbals are completely different.

Once I was on a team at work where I really enjoyed what we were doing and also the people on the team. I was a bit surprised when the team leader approached me and asked me why I was always upset during the meetings. I had no idea that I was giving this impression to other people. What I learned was that when my mind was engaged in problem solving, I tended to lean back, cross my arms, look up at the ceiling and frown. Unfortunately, my colleagues saw my non-verbal behavior and naturally assumed I was disengaged and angry. From then on I learned to adopt a new "problem solving pose" that included leaning forward, maintaining eye contact with whoever was speaking, and making sure I wasn't frowning while I was thinking!

Practice Session: Identifying Warmth

For the next day, pay attention to the greetings you receive in *all* your interactions (at home, at work, at the gas station, at the drive-thru where you get lunch, etc.) and notice who gives you a warm greeting and who doesn't give you a warm greeting.

Describe the non-verbal behavior in the warm greetings…

Describe the non-verbal behavior in the greetings that lacked warmth…

Where We Lose Our Warmth

We get very mixed up when it comes to warmth because we confuse the roles of warmth and genuineness. Perhaps on your way into work your mom called to try to guilt you into visiting her. You are also worried about how you're going to pay your bills this week, and the "check engine" light on your dashboard comes on. You are in a bad mood. Wouldn't it be phony to smile and greet people with a warm "hello"? Isn't it more genuine to be grumpy and miserable?

Here is the problem. When we have this "I'm just being real" mindset, we are missing the fact that genuineness is about *us*, while warmth is about *others*. Genuineness is about how I'm feeling; warmth is about how valuable you are to me.

When someone has the ability to consistently express warmth to you, it lets you know that your value to them doesn't depend on how they are feeling. When you develop the ability to consistently express warmth to others, it lets them know that their value to you doesn't depend on how you are feeling. This is why being treated with warmth is a non-negotiable: because being valued is a non-negotiable. If one person in a relationship does not consistently value the other, there is literally nothing on which to build a healthy connection. This leads to another axiom for loving well:

Warmth equals value, so warmth is a non-negotiable.

Remember that in this first stage the over-arching theme is having the ability to always act like there are two separate people in the relationship who are equally valuable and equally powerful. When someone lacks the ability to consistently be warm towards you, they are in essence saying, "Sometimes I am so caught up in myself that I can't be bothered with treating you like you have value to me. Your value will rise and fall depending on my mood and my circumstances."

As you work on tuning your people picker, warmth is a critical thing to pay attention to. People who value you will be consistent with their warmth. They will be warm when they are going through good times and when they are going through tough times. They will be warm when you say yes to what they want and warm when you say no. They will be warm when you agree with them, and just as warm when you disagree. Their warmth doesn't change because your value doesn't change, and they have the ability to realize you are a separate person.

The Wrong Approach

Sometimes when someone is not expressing warmth we make the mistake of taking responsibility for their emotional state and we try to get them to a place where they can be warm. If they are not warm because they are sad we try to cheer them up. If they are not warm because they are irritated we try to calm them down. There are two huge problems with this. The first, and this is the biggest one, is we are buying into the belief that "it is my job to get you to a place where you treat me like I matter to you." If you want a recipe for a lifetime of misery, this is it. It is never your job to get people to value you. It is your job to *pay attention* to the people who consistently value you through their actions and invest in those relationships, and *pay attention* to the people who do not consistently value you through their actions and limit or end those relationships.

The second problem with trying to change others' emotional states is we are confusing emotions and warmth. It's possible to be angry and warm at the same time. It's possible to be sad and warm at the same time. It's possible to let someone know that you are glad to see them and at the same time let them know you are having a tough day. That is because your emotions are about you and warmth is about their value, and both can be true at the same time. When you come home at the end of a tough day, you can choose not to greet your spouse, not make eye contact, and walk around grumbling; or, you can walk in and give your spouse a big hug and say "Nice to see you, honey. You wouldn't believe the day I had."

In a good relationship, we do not have to take turns having value (when I'm sad I can act like you don't exist and when you're angry you can act like I don't matter). Value can remain a constant while emotions go up and down.

Solving the Problem

Sometimes when we discover that we are not treating others with warmth it's just because we have developed bad habits, as I did with my "problem solving pose" that my colleagues interpreted as annoyance. If this is the case it's a pretty simple fix. We need to start adopting non-verbal behaviors that match what is really going on in our heart.

But other times the problem is much deeper. Other times the reason we don't express warmth is that we truly don't value the people we interact with each day. Or, more accurately, we do not value them in the manner that God values them. We might value them for what they do for us, but we do not see them as one of God's masterpieces. In this case our non-verbals really do match what is going on in our heart, so it is our heart that needs to change. For this reason I have discovered that expressing warmth is one of the most basic spiritual disciplines, because it helps us align our hearts with God's heart.

Sometimes the reason we don't value others properly is because there is something about ourselves that we value more. Often, for example, we value our pain and hardship more than we value other people. When we see others all our non-verbals are about *us*. Our misery has eclipsed the other person's value and so we don't even think about expressing warmth. This is another reason warmth is such a great spiritual discipline, because it helps us to focus on valuing others equally to ourselves.

Personal Reflection: Warmth

Think about a relationship were the other person consistently treated you with warmth. How did that impact the relationship? How did that impact the way you felt about yourself?

Think about a relationship were the other person consistently demonstrated a lack of warmth. How did that impact the relationship? How did that impact the way you felt about yourself?

Practice Session: Prayer and/or Meditation

If you believe in God, ask him to give you his heart for each person you interact with each day. Ask him to show you who you have been judging, who you have been ignoring, and who you have been taking for granted. If you don't believe in God or do not pray, for the next week spend time reflecting on who you have been judging, who you have been ignoring, and who you have been taking for granted.

Journal your thoughts as you prayed or reflected this week. What did you discover?

When Warmth is Not Possible

Are there moments in life when we just cannot express warmth? Absolutely. Sometimes we are so overwhelmed by physical or emotional pain that we truly are unable to get outside of ourselves and treat others with warmth. But there are two things to keep in mind about these exceptions. The first is that even though we cannot express warmth it is still our responsibility to treat others with warmth! In other words, it is our job to explain to others what is going on. If you are going into a team meeting at work and you have a migraine, it is your job to say "Hey gang, I've got a splitting headache. So if I seem a little grumpy, that's probably why." When you do this then people don't have to wonder about your non-verbal clues and what they mean.

The second thing to keep in mind is that if you want to build healthy relationships these moments need to be few and far between. If someone consistently has an excuse for not being warm then there is a deeper issue that they need to solve before they can begin building real connections with others. I cannot overstress this point. You can feel empathy for people who have no warmth, but you cannot build a relationship with them. You can pray for them, but you can't have a great dating relationship with them or build a strong marriage with them.

Conversely, if you have difficulty consistently expressing warmth to others then there is a deeper issue that you need to take responsibility for before you can love well and connect deeply. You may need to talk to a doctor or counselor to discover the challenges you have in consistently expressing warmth to others. You owe it to yourself to discover and heal whatever has been preventing you from consistently treating others with warmth, because without this you will never be able to sustain a relationship that is life-giving and satisfies your heart.

Practice Session: Expressing Warmth

Warmth is expressing to others through words, tone of voice, and body language *that they are valuable to you.*

Warmth is something we want to express throughout our time with others, but a good place to focus when you are starting out is expressing warmth when you are greeting others. For an entire day, try to give everyone you interact with a warm greeting. This means the people you live with and the people you work with. It means the cashier at the gas station and the person at the drive-thru where you get lunch. It means the receptionist at the dentist's office and your daughter's soccer coach. It can be a simple "Hi," "Good to see you" or "How's it going?" The words are not as important as your non-verbal greeting. Pay special attention to making eye contact, smiling, and letting your warmth be reflected in your tone of voice.

In what situations was it easy for you to express warmth?

In what situations was it more difficult for you to express warmth?

How did it make you feel when you were able to express warmth to others?

Practice Session: Expressing Warmth

Another good place to focus when you are starting out is

expressing warmth when you are saying goodbye to others. For an entire day, try to give everyone you interact with a warm goodbye. It can be a simple "Have a great day," "Have a nice night" or "It was great to see you." Once again, the words are not as important as your non-verbal expressions. Pay special attention to making eye contact, smiling, and letting your warmth be reflected in your tone of voice.

In what situations was it easy for you to express warmth?

In what situations was it more difficult for you to express warmth?

How did it make you feel when you were able to express warmth to others?

Listening with warmth: Mirroring

Now that you have practiced expressing warmth in your greetings and goodbyes, let's practice expressing warmth in conversations. Just as with greetings and goodbyes, the warmth (and therefore the value) that you communicate is done primarily through your non-verbal communication. Your facial expressions, tone of voice, and body language will still be your key tools, but this time there is a critical difference. Instead of focusing on smiling, which communicates value in greetings and goodbyes, it more helpful to try to mirror the emotion that the person is communicating. If someone is communicating sadness, you can value that sadness by making sure your facial expressions and tone of voice mirror the pain they are feeling. When someone expresses anger, you can value that with facial expressions and tone of voice that mirror their concerns. If someone is communicating excitement you can mirror their delight in your face and vocal tones to let them know you value their happiness. Usually it is most helpful if our mirroring is less intense than what we see in others. If we match their intensity level we can accidently rob them of the chance to express their feelings.

When we fail to mirror another person's emotions it is very difficult for them to experience that we value what they are going through. If they are expressing sadness and we have a blank look on our face, or if they express happiness our non-verbals suggest that we are angry, it is very easy for them to feel devalued.

Personal Reflection: In your conversations with family, friends, and colleagues over the next few days, try to pay attention to the warmth expressed by the people you are talking to you. Do you get the sense that they are engaged and eager to listen to what you have to say? Or, do you get the sense that they are uninterested or even annoyed? What specifically in their body language, facial expressions and tone of voice communicated their interest level?

Pick one conversation this week and plan on paying attention to your non-verbal communication to express that value you place on having the chance to listen to this person. Pay special attention to mirroring the emotional content of their communication with your facial expressions and tone of voice. Do this one or two times a week for the next few weeks.

Getting Feedback: After practicing this for a few weeks, ask someone to give you feedback about the warmth you have expressed when listening to them. Here are some questions you can ask them.

When you are talking to me, do you sense that I value the chance to listen to you?

What specifically do I do to make you think that I am interested or uninterested?

What is one specific thing that I could do to better communicate that I value the chance to hear what you are thinking and feeling?

Red Flag: There are a lot of people in the world who are smart, funny, fun, good looking, rich, successful…but lack warmth. As appealing as some of these other characteristics can be, they are not enough to overcome a lack of warmth. You will have a much richer life if you choose to connect with people who treat you with value every time they see you than wasting years trying to make a cold person happy enough to treat you with warmth.

10 Appreciation

Pleasant words are a honeycomb, sweet to the soul and healing to the bones.
Proverbs 16:24

How would you like to go to bed tonight knowing that today you made two or three people feel loved who hadn't felt loved in a long time? How would you like to have that experience day after day, week after week, leaving a wake behind you of people who feel touched at a human level and who have a little bit more hope and energy to face the challenges of life?

In this chapter we are going to talk about a simple tool that you can have in your relational tool belt to do just that. It's free. It's easy. It doesn't take long. But it's also largely ignored. One time I was leading a management seminar with about 40 managers. I asked them to each write down ten recent instances that one of their direct reports did an important task or job exactly the way they wanted it done. When each had finished their list, I then asked them to put a check by each instance in which they let the employee know that they had done the task perfectly. For 36 of the managers the answer was zero! These managers were not only missing out on an opportunity to reinforce the behavior that they wanted, they were missing out on a chance to appreciate the people working for them.

Most of us are trying to do our best in life, but very few of us feel appreciated for what we do. It's easy to feel taken for granted. But it's just as easy to take others for granted and forget that they are also trying to do their best with little appreciation. Perhaps it's because we get so little appreciation we treat it as a scarce commodity.

Appreciation is an essential part of helping people understand and feel their value. Just as warmth is a way of letting others know that we value who they are, appreciation is a way of letting others know that we value the impact that they have on our lives.

I believe that most people have great hearts and want the people in their lives to feel appreciated, but once again what we lack is the skill to accomplish this. Most of us have never had a lesson on how to appreciate. Fortunately, it's a simple skill to learn and you can begin practicing it immediately.

How to show appreciation

There are three parts to helping people feel appreciated:

1) Talk about the specific behavior you appreciate
2) Talk about how the behavior impacts you
3) Talk about the character trait you see in that behavior

Specific and concrete

The first way to help someone feel appreciated is to describe the specific behavior that you appreciate in concrete language. Instead of using vague generalizations like "You're doing a great job!" or "You're an awesome worker!" or "You're a great friend", describe the specific behavior or actions that you noticed which made you think these generalizations are true.

I am fascinated by the fact that we all want to be appreciated, yet at the same time most of us have the habit of minimizing or downright rejecting appreciation when it comes our way. If you tell someone "You're a great mom" she is likely to say something self-depreciating like "I've got you fooled!" or "You should see me at the end of a long day – you wouldn't say that!"

Even if she doesn't say something like that, it is very likely she is thinking something similar, so the compliment doesn't reach her heart. Because of this almost universal human reaction, if you want to help people feel appreciated you need to make it rejection-proof! The first way to make the appreciation rejection-proof is to avoid vague language.

If you tell someone "You're doing a great job" then they can automatically think about the areas where they're really struggling and the six things they did wrong this week, and the appreciation is lost. But if you say "We've had ten emails in the last two weeks from customers complimenting you on your service," then there is no way they can argue with that (assuming it's true!). If you tell someone "You're a great dad" then he can dismiss it as politeness. But if you say "That's the second time I've seen one of your kids spill their drink, and I noticed each time you didn't raise your voice or lose your temper, you just patiently helped them clean up their mess," then he can't deny or minimize what you are saying.

It makes a difference

The second part of helping people feel appreciated is let them know how the specific behavior you described makes a positive impact in your life. There are several ways that someone's behavior can impact you in positive way.

The impact can be ***practical:***
That helped me get my job finished on time…
That helped us stay under budget…
I was able to attend my son's basketball game…
That allowed me to take the weekend off…

The impact can be ***emotional:***

That really encouraged me...
I felt relaxed the rest of the day...
I felt proud to be your dad...
That inspired me to keep going myself...
I felt comforted and not so alone...

The impact can be ***relational*:**
That was a trust builder for me...
I felt more connected to you...
That really helped me know you...
That made me believe I can be honest about my opinions
with you...

Notice the change here. When we talked about the behavior we appreciate we were talking about something that *they* did. Now we are not talking about *them*, but about *us*. We are talking about how we feel, what we believe, or what we were able to do or experience because of their behavior. We are using "I" language. This is important because it's another way that we make appreciation rejection-proof and help them to feel the appreciation. If I say that your actions "inspired everybody" or "You're an encouraging person," then you could probably dismiss that pretty easily. But if I say they inspired *me* or encouraged *me* then you can't argue with that, because I'm the expert on what I feel and believe!

I see a trend here

The final part of helping people feel appreciated is to point out the positive character trait that you see behind their behavior.

I think you are a very thoughtful and supportive friend.
To me, that's another example of how honest you are.

That's one of the reasons I see you as a safe person.
I get the impression that integrity is very important to you.

Again, it's important to be specific and to use "I" language when you do this. If you tell someone that they have a strong work ethic it can be easily dismissed, but if you tell them *you believe* they have a strong work ethic they can't argue with you that you believe that, and they will go to bed that night with the knowledge that someone in the world believes that they have a strong work ethic!

Here, too, it's helpful to be specific. Telling someone you believe that they are trustworthy or loyal or generous is more impactful than saying that you believe they are a "great guy" or "good person."

Genuineness: the essential ingredient

Showing appreciation is not a method to butter people up, nor is it a schmaltzy way to make people feel good. Showing appreciation is a way to value people by letting them know the positive ways they impact your life and what you think that says about their character. Because of this, genuineness is the single most important ingredient to showing appreciation. It would be better to give a sincere but vague "You're a great friend" than give a more concrete and thought out appreciation if you didn't really believe it. In the long run people can usually tell when they are being manipulated, and insincere appreciation will end up creating a barrier between you and others rather than creating relationship.

Barriers to showing appreciation

I think the biggest barrier to helping others feel appreciated is simply that we have never learned how to do it well. But there are a couple of other attitude shifts we may need to make in order to get better at showing appreciation.

The first shift is a shift in focus. Everyone you meet is a mixed bag. They have strong points and weak points. They do things that annoy you or put you off, and they do things that you appreciate and even admire. We can tend to focus on others' negative behaviors and traits to the point that we don't see their strengths. Worse, we can feel justified in not appreciating their strengths. In order to truly appreciate others, you may have to shift your focus to see both the weaknesses and the strengths. By the way, there is a side benefit to this: when you grow in your ability to appreciate others' strengths despite their weaknesses, it will also help you appreciate your own strengths despite your many weaknesses.

The second barrier is a little more insidious. Sometimes we feel in competition in our relationships. We keep score. We may think "If I tell you how much I appreciate something about you, that may give the impression that you are winning – and you are definitely not winning! You are not the better employee, or brother, or spouse!" We are afraid that appreciating others will elevate them and put us in an inferior position. There is a little bit of truth to this. It sometimes takes humility and vulnerability to tell someone they are making a positive difference in your life. And if you did this just once it might create a lingering sense of inferiority. But if you regularly show appreciation it's a different story. Appreciation is relational gold, and the person who shows up at the office or home or bar and regularly passes out gold will be seen as the person with real power.

Practice Session:

In the following scenarios try to focus on the strengths and let the person know how much you appreciate them. Make sure you describe specific behavior and use "I" statements.

1. You work second shift at a restaurant. One of the employees on first shift rubs you the wrong way. It's probably because she rarely smiles or laughs, and she seems a bit too uptight. But she always has her section cleaned and stocked before she leaves, and never leaves any of her tasks for others to do. If the day has been exceptionally busy she will even stay later than scheduled to make sure the next shift is set up for success.

Describe the behavior:

Describe how it impacts you:

Talk about the positive character trait:

2. Your elementary school-aged son is not the best student, and he struggles to do his chores consistently. But you have also noticed that he makes friends easily. Whenever there is a new kid at school or church, or a kid who seems to have a hard time fitting in, your son is the first person to talk to him and helps him feel included.

Describe what you notice: — I notice how quickly/easily you circle around those who might ~~feet~~ feel on the outside

Describe how it impacts you: — That really makes me feel good, as I often feel on the outside

Talk about the positive character trait: encourager feels safe

I think you are a wonderful includer, helper ~~that every whenever you~~ with the people around you

3. Your husband has been spending more time at work than you would like, and even when he comes home he seems to have work on the brain. But you also notice that on the nights he cooks dinner he has been very conscientious about making meals that follow the guidelines you talked to him about when you began training to run a marathon. Not only that, he seems to put some extra effort into making sure the dinners are delicious!

Describe what you notice:

Describe how it impacts you:

Talk about the positive character trait:

4. Your boss has always struck you as just a little bit flighty, and you wish she would communicate her expectations more clearly. But she also has given you several assignments in the last year that have given you a chance to gain the critical experience you need to be promoted someday. She also consistently praises your work in front of her supervisors.

Describe what you notice:

Describe how it impacts you:

Talk about the positive character trait:

Practice Session:

Now that you have practiced with some hypothetical situations, let's apply this tool closer to home. Think about three people in your life that you appreciate. It could be members of your immediate family, friends, or coworkers. It could be volunteers at your church, synagogue or mosque. Take a moment and write out an appreciation for each one, making sure that you are using specific examples of what you appreciate and using "I" language. After you write them out, we'll talk about different ways to share them.

1. Name: *A.*

Describe what you notice: — *You really notice that you really like to do things correctly.*

Describe how it impacts you: — *~~That really~~ I really value that because it shows that you want to honor and do a great job.*

Talk about the positive character trait: *That shows me that you ~~really value~~ a person of integrity.*

2. Name:

Describe what you notice:

Describe how it impacts you:

Talk about the positive character trait:

3. Name:

Describe what you notice:

Describe how it impacts you:

Talk about the positive character trait:

Getting Personal

One thing you will notice about showing appreciation is it can be a deeply personal experience. When you show appreciation to others it can touch a deep place in their hearts. If you feel a little awkward the first time you tell someone what you appreciate about them then you are not alone. It can feel so personal that you might be tempted to skip it altogether! I have found it helpful to begin by saying something like "Hey Mary, can I share something with you?" or "Mike, can I tell you something fun I've noticed?" The good news is, once we have broken the ice and showed appreciation the first time, it changes the relationship a little bit. In a world where it is easy to dehumanize one another and feel like cogs in a machine, when you show appreciation to someone it suddenly feels like there are two real, live human beings in the room – and my experience is that this shift is usually long lasting. Share one appreciation with someone who has always felt like a stranger at work, even with someone that you think doesn't like you very much, and see how much more personal and friendly the relationship feels afterwards.

Another option is to send your words of appreciation in a card or email. My mother-in-law, Ruth, is the queen at showing appreciation through note cards, and I'm guessing it is one of the reasons she seems to have so many friends and acquaintances. Emails are also a fun way to show appreciation because the person can read it over and over again.

One final suggestion: A great way to show appreciation to others in the business world is to tell their boss or company how much you appreciate them. Whenever my wife gets great service at a grocery or department store she not only thanks the employee but tries to find a manager to let them know how much she appreciates what the employee did for her. She will also get on the corporate website to let the company know how much the service meant to her, making sure to identify the employee by name.

Personal Reflection: After you have shared the three appreciations from the above exercise, reflect on the experience. What was it like to share your appreciation with that person? How do you think it impacted that person to hear your words of appreciation?

Practice Session: Make a list of 50 people in your life that you haven't expressed appreciation towards lately. Start paying attention to the positive things about them and the way these positive things impact you. Try to write and share one or two appreciations each week.

Red Flag: When looking to take a relationship to the next level, pay attention to how the person treats people who are part of his everyday world. This can include the many strangers he may meet like restaurant servers, cashiers, and sales clerks. Is he appreciative of the service that they provide? Does he thank them? Is he personable with them or does he treat them like cogs in the machine? It can also include people he sees more regularly, like his co-workers or employees. Does he take for granted the work they do or does he value the effort that they put into their job? What does he do and say to make sure these people feel appreciated? The behavior he demonstrates towards them can be a preview of how he will treat you when you are a regular part of his life. You do not want to get trapped in a significant relationship with someone who does not have the ability or the desire to appreciate others.

Part Three:

Loving Well by Protecting Others' Power

11 Respect

Show proper respect to everyone, love the family of believers,
fear God, honor the emperor.
1 Peter 2:17

If we want to use our hearts to love others well, it is absolutely critical that we learn both the attitudes and the skills necessary to communicate respect to each person we meet. There are three different kinds of respect that we can have towards another person, so it is important to define which one we are talking about in this context.

Perhaps at work there is someone whose expertise or judgment has proven helpful time and time again, and so when she offers her input people tend to listen more attentively. Or perhaps you know a teacher who has quietly sacrificed for many years so that his students have every chance of getting into college, and so you esteem him in a special way. This kind of respect is *earned* respect. This is the respect that comes from someone demonstrating such character or competency that our admiration for them increases over time.

A second kind of respect is a respect for someone's office or position. It's the kind of respect that we would show the president of the United States if we were to meet him, whether or not we agree with his political policies. It's the kind of respect we would show a police officer while he is performing his duties. We may have never met him and have no idea whether he is a good man or not, but that is irrelevant. It's not the person we are showing respect to but the badge or the office.

In this chapter we are not talking about either of these kinds of respect. We are talking about what I call *core respect*. It is the respect that all persons deserve simply because they are human beings. Before we move on to talking about how specifically to demonstrate this core respect to others, I want to talk about some challenges we face in showing respect.

People are different

Here is a significant challenge we face in our attempt to use our hearts to love well: People are different, and they are different in so many ways.

People have different beliefs. We have different political beliefs ranging from far left to moderate to far right and every stop in between. We have different religious beliefs: from theism to deism to dualism to agnosticism to atheism (and wide variations in each category). We have different beliefs in philosophy and ethics. We have different beliefs about history. Take any field of science and you will find rich and fertile debate as new questions are explored, and as new discoveries challenge held beliefs.

People have different opinions. We have different opinions about whoever the current president is and how he is performing, and just as many different opinions about whoever the current coach of our favorite college or pro sports team is and how he is performing. We have different opinions about who is the greatest basketball player right now, or who is the greatest of all time. We have different opinions about how to best impact our local economy, or whether the local school system's budget should be increased or decreased.

People have different values. When I say that people have different values what I really mean is that we rank our values differently. If you ask anyone if they value loyalty or honesty or family or their country or personal freedom they will most probably say yes. The real differences come in how we rank our values. Life forces us to make hard choices, and these choices force us to decide what we value the most. Some of us value loyalty over honesty and will hide the truth to protect a friend. Others of us with different values will do the exact opposite in the same situation. Some of us value our careers over having a family; others of us will value family over having a career.

People have different tastes. We have different tastes in food, with some of us loving seafood, others of us hating it, and still others of us can take it or leave it. We have different tastes in music: name any current musical act and you will find some people who love them and others who have to turn the radio off when they come on. We have different tastes in dress and personal style. We have different tastes in what we find funny. We have different taste in literature.

And the list goes on and on. People make different moral choices, have different goals, different cultural backgrounds, different talents, different wants and different hobbies.

People are different, and they are different in so many ways.

Conformity vs. Respect

One of the things that will have a huge impact on your ability to get to know others and build friendships is whether, in a world where people are so different in so many ways, you value conformity or respect more highly. These are two completely different attitudes and they lead to two completely different ways of relating.

When we value conformity most highly, then we tend to have one overriding concern when we are getting to know people: *Are you like me?* And when we listen with the "Are you like me?" concern we are by default listening to critique, categorize, evaluate and judge. We are listening to divide into groups, to create opposite camps. We are engaging in a process that is, by its very nature, disconnecting rather than connecting. Further, when we value conformity most highly, we tend to assume that if someone is not like us it is because they have some defect. We tend to caricature and demonize those who are not like us. Go on any website where different views are expressed (it doesn't matter whether it is about politics, religion, music, or sports) and within the first few entries you will find people dividing into sides, with each side calling the other side "morons" or "idiots" or some other insult. When we value conformity we tend to think "I will treat you with respect if you are like me: if you think like me, act like me, dress like me, and talk like me." Conformity is critical and respect is negotiable.

We can make a different choice, however. In a world where people are different in so many ways, we can choose to value respect over conformity. When we value respect most highly, then we have a different overriding concern when getting to know people. Instead of asking "Are you like me?" we wonder *"Who are you and what makes you uniquely you?"* When we value respect we go beyond categories. Discovering that someone is a Democrat or Republican is enough to categorize them, but not to understand them. So we listen to understand *why* they are a Democrat or Republican. What values and beliefs drive their political choices? At what age did they become a Democrat or Republican? Are they more concerned about social issues or economic issues, or do they weigh them each equally? Did any prominent political figure create their loyalty? There are a host of questions that we could ask that would each give us a fuller picture of this unique person.

This heightened value for conformity over respect is challenging enough when it comes to groups like the book club or the softball team, but it is absolutely fatal for any church that wants to reflect the vision and values of Jesus. One of the most striking and unexpected characteristics of Jesus is his unwavering respect for individuals and his low value for conformity. One theme we see in all four gospels in the New Testament is the ongoing conflict that Jesus had with the Pharisees. The Pharisees had an extremely high value for conformity. They believed they had the right answer for any question, and were highly critical of anyone who didn't believe or behave the way that they did. Jesus, on the other hand, would initiate relationship with anybody. He would engage them in conversation. He would eat and drink and party with them. He would invite himself over for dinner. And all indications are that they didn't feel judged or evaluated but enjoyed and loved. This infuriated the Pharisees, who believed it was their job to let everyone know where they were falling short.

Respect and the races we run

I can be very judgmental, and my judgments can be very cruel and thoughtless. I can form snap judgments on the people that I meet based on the way they dress, the way they talk, how they spend their money, their moral decisions, how they choose to entertain themselves, how they treat their children, and a host of other reasons. What is worse, my negative judgment allows me to believe that I don't have to treat that person with respect.

I wonder if one of the reasons Jesus was able to treat each person with respect is because he was so aware that, in life, we are not all running the same race. We don't all have the same starting line, the same finish line, or the same obstacles on our course. Some of the people you meet today grew up in homes where they were always safe and loved. Others you meet grew up in homes where they were abused by the very people who were supposed to help them feel valued and protected. Some people you meet today grew up surrounded by parents, grandparents, and aunts and uncles who all adored them. Others you meet have never heard the words "I love you" and don't know what it feels like to have people who care about them. These are very different starting lines.

Some of the people you meet today went to good schools with competent and attentive teachers, and had parents who paid attention to their school work and helped them grow and learn. Other people you meet went to schools that were overcrowded and underfunded and had parents who were too overwhelmed by their own addictions to even notice what was happening with the child's schoolwork. Some of the people you meet came from homes with narcissistic parents who only saw their children as reflections of themselves; while others came from families who were determined to help each of her children realize their unique potential. Some of the people you meet got plenty of attention just for being themselves; and others only got attention when they were seductive or destructive or depressed. Some people you meet have been bullied horribly, some have experienced devastating losses, and some have had every advantage one could hope for. These are very different obstacles.

We also have no idea what the finish line of each person we meet is going to look like. We have all read stories of people who have dramatically changed the course of their lives by overcoming things like hatred, racism, indifference or addictions and have ended up making a significant contribution to the lives of others. We have also read stories of people who have met with initial and overwhelming success whose lives spiraled into self-destructive behavior and who ended up doing great damage to themselves and others. These are very different finish lines.

I believe we can also add a divine dimension to this. When we give our lives and even our pain to God, he gives our lives a new purpose. He draws a new finish line. He uses everything about us – our strengths and weaknesses, our successes and failures, the things of which we are most proud and most ashamed, our greatest advantages and our greatest disadvantages – in order to bring His love and hope to others.

You may meet someone whom you think that you are a mile ahead of in life, but you don't know if their starting line was twenty miles behind yours. And you don't know what kind of obstacles they have had to overcome to get where they are now. And since you don't know what race God may ask them to run, you don't know where their finish line will be. You may have had a relatively easy sprint to run in life, and that may be perfect for the purpose God has for you. But someone else may have a long, obstacle-filled marathon, and that may suit God's purpose for their life. God is at work trying to draw *all men and women* to Himself: the powerful and the powerless, the rich and the poor, the healthy and the sick, the free and the imprisoned – and people stuck in every kind of destructive lifestyle imaginable. We each have a different race that prepares us to understand and relate to the people that God uses us to love with His love. I'm guessing that some people I'm tempted to disrespect or belittle are people that God will use to run a heroic race that would crush me if I were to attempt it.

When I remember this it keeps me sober and helps me to focus on running my race as best as I can and not try to guess what kind of race others are running or how well they are doing. It makes me more interested in being curious about what their life has been like and what has brought them to the point they are at today.

Curiosity vs. Judgment

You can have one of two postures when you meet people: you can be curious to know them or you can be eager to judge them. You can do one or the other, but you can't do both.

When we value respect over conformity it frees us up to be

curious about the people we meet. The curious person realizes there is a lot under the surface of each person he talks to each day. We are all made up of a myriad of memories, struggles, losses, hopes, decisions, promises, defense mechanisms, and defining moments. The judgmental person tends to see only what is on the surface; the curious person wants to know how the person became the person they are today.

Here is one small example. I have a friend named Scott who is a Miami Dolphins fan. This is a bit unexpected, since he is a lifetime resident of Ohio and is a big fan of the Buckeyes and Reds. Why the Dolphins? Why isn't he a Bengal fan? For a judgmental person that might be enough to judge Scott as a fair weather fan. After all, historically it's been a bit easier to be a Buckeyes or Reds fan than it has been to be a Bengals fan!

But the curious person wouldn't be satisfied with a surface explanation, and so might ask Scott how he became a fan of the Dolphins. If he asked, Scott would tell him that when he was young he went with his father to the NFL Hall of Fame. At one point his father pointed to a man and said "You might want to get his autograph." When Scott asked for the autograph, the man shook his hand (at this point Scott will demonstrate how the man's hand was so huge that his own hand completely disappeared) and told Scott he would give him an autograph if Scott promised to be a Dolphin fan for life. Scott agreed that he would, and Larry Csonka gave Scott his autograph. Scott has been a loyal Dolphin fan to this day, keeping the promise he made to one of the legends of the NFL.

Life is a lot more fun when we stop making automatic, surface judgments of others and are open to seeing what lies beneath. The people we meet, even the people who live and believe very differently, become more three dimensional and more human. If you want to have some fun, get in the habit of asking people how they became a fan of their favorite team. You will hear fun and sometimes touching stories about their grandfathers, or vacations they took when they were young, or their first time at a major league game, or how sitting with their dad every Sunday afternoon watching the game was one of the highlights of childhood. You will hear very human and connecting stories.

And if you can take a posture of curiosity instead of judgment, you will hear the same human and connecting stories when you ask people why they became a Republican or Democrat or Buddhist or atheist or Christian; or why they decided to go into medicine or law or culinary arts; or why that particular author is their favorite, or why they always go to that certain place for their vacation. People can generally sense when you are asking to judge and when you are asking because you genuinely want to know the human being beneath the surface, no matter how different they may be from you, and no matter how you might disagree with their thinking. You can use your mind to evaluate other people's thinking and at the same time use your heart to connect with them as a fellow human being trying to figure out life in all of its complexity.

Respect and Separateness

Remember, in this first stage of building relationships we are focusing on maintaining awareness that there are two separate people who each have equal value and power. When one person becomes less valuable or less powerful than the other, then there is no way for the relationship to thrive. Here is another axiom that will help you learn how to use your heart to love well:

Respect is a non-negotiable, because respect is the attitude that maintains the separateness and power of each person in the relationship.

There are different kinds of power, and some of them are unequal. Some people have more financial power than others, and sometimes we have more financial power at one point in our lives and less in others. Some people have more political power than others for a season, and then when they leave office all of their political power is gone. We can have more positional power than some people at work and less positional power than others, and this also can fluctuate. This is not the kind of power we are talking about.

We are talking about personal power, which is always equal and always unchanging between adults who are in relationship. It includes the power to choose our own beliefs, opinions, values, tastes, goals and wants. It includes the power to make our own choices and reap the consequences of those choices.

When there are two people in a relationship who have equal power, they each get to formulate their own thoughts, have their own opinions, embrace their own values, enjoy their own tastes, and make their own choices without it impacting the level of core respect with which they are treated. It's okay to decide not to marry someone who makes choices you do not approve of. It's okay not to go into business with someone whose values are out of kilter with yours. But it is not okay to withhold core respect from them.

Red Flag: If you are in a relationship with someone who will treat you with respect only as long as you agree with him, respect has become negotiable, and there is no way you can be a separate, powerful person. In fact, there is really no way you can have a relationship with him because he has decided there is only room for one real person in the relationship. Only one person gets to think, have opinions, or decide which values are important.

Personal Reflection: What criteria do you tend to use to judge people? Why do you think you use those specific criteria?

If someone were to observe the way you treat others, do you think they would come to the conclusion that you value conformity or respect more highly? What would lead them to this conclusion?

How many solid, respect-filled relationships do you have with people who are different from you in many important areas? Why do you think that is?

12 Listening with Respect

...knowledge puffs up while love builds up.
1 Corinthians 8:1

It's one thing to have a desire to treat others with the core respect that they deserve, and it's another thing to have the ability to communicate that respect to them. In this chapter we are going to learn and practice the primary skill you need to have in order to consistently treat others with respect, and thus be able to build relationship with them while helping to preserve their value and power as separate people. Fortunately, we have already learned the first two steps we need to know in order to practice this skill. Unfortunately we have some major mental barriers to overcome – and bad habits to unlearn – in order to use this skill consistently. We'll deal with the skill building first, and as we do so, pay attention to any inner conflict you feel!

Skill Building

We have already learned to listen with empathy in order to understand what is going on in other people's relationships with the people and things that they love. We are now going to use that skill to learn how to listen with respect, so that we can understand who people are and what makes them unique individuals.

We learned three steps to listening with empathy:

1. Identifying the feeling
2. Identifying the thought

3. Reflecting both the feeling and thought back to the speaker in a tentative statement.

It sounds like you are relieved to hear that you don't have to do jury duty.

Are you saying that you are frightened by the way he was talking to you?

Sometimes when we are communicating things like beliefs, opinions, values, and choices, there is no emotional content to the statement. So we are going to modify the way we listen, and then add a few new steps.

1. Identify the thought.
2. Reflect the thought back to the speaker in a tentative statement.
3. Identify the value behind the thought.
4. Reflect the value back to the speaker in a tentative sentence.
5. Affirm the value.

Here is an example.

Speaker: *I think it's absolutely critical to take a family vacation every year. The time away helps everyone to de-stress, and the memories that you make on vacation last a lifetime. It helps everyone to feel more connected with one another, and gives time for conversations that don't always happen when you are in the busyness of day to day life.*

1. Identify the thought: Vacations are important for a family.

2. Reflect the thought back to the speaker in a tentative statement: *Sounds like you believe that family vacations are pretty critical.*

Speaker: *Absolutely. I think they're one of the most important times a family has together.*

3. Identify the value behind the thought: feeling connected as a family.

4. Reflect the value back to the speaker in a tentative sentence: *It sounds like you have a high value for helping everyone in your family feel connected to one another.*

Speaker: *Yeah, that's always been important to me.*

5. Affirm the value: *That's a great thing to value. I can see how that must have a great impact on your family.*

If you can get to the point where you have understood the value behind a belief or opinion, then you can reach a point of connection with the speaker. This is true even if you disagree with the belief or opinion itself, or the reasoning behind the belief or opinion. Let's look at an example that can sometimes be a little bit more challenging for some of us.

Speaker: *I think the Bible is just a bunch of man-made myths. Besides that, it has probably changed a lot as it has been copied through the centuries. Who knows what it said originally? If you put your trust in the Bible you're just deciding to bury your head in the sand and ignore reality.*

1. Identify the thought: The Bible is unreliable.

2. Reflect the thought back to the speaker in a tentative statement: *Sounds like you think the Bible is not very credible.*

Speaker: *No. It might have some nice ideas, but that doesn't mean it is the word of God.*

3. Identify the value behind the thought: honest skepticism

4. Reflect the value back to the speaker in a tentative sentence: *It sounds like you have a high value for intellectual integrity – making sure what you believe is really true.*

Speaker: *It's the only honest way to live.*

5. Affirm the value: *I think that's a really a great value to have.*

It's important to note here that there is a big difference between *reflecting* the thought and *caricaturing* the thought. When we reflect back someone's thought we are paraphrasing it in a way that they would agree with. When we caricature someone's thought we are paraphrasing it in a way to make it sound ridiculous. Let's look at two examples of caricaturing.

Speaker: *I believe that we were created by an all-powerful, loving God.*

Listener: *So, you believe in a magical genie who just blinks his eyes and makes things exist?*

Speaker: *I believe that we evolved through a process of natural selection from lower life forms.*

Listener: *So, you think we are really just a bunch of monkeys who should be swinging in trees?*

Few things are more disrespectful than caricaturing someone's thoughts, yet much of what passes for conversation these days involves a lot of caricature. When you caricature someone's thoughts you are communicating a lack of respect for them as a person and are also communicating that you have no desire to understand what they are saying. Loving people well involves taking the time to understand others' thoughts *from their perspective* whether you agree with them or not.

Red Flag: Be very careful about investing in a relationship with someone who consistently caricatures viewpoints he doesn't agree with. Needing to distort or parody someone else's ideas betrays a lack of intellectual integrity and curiosity. The high level of disrespect and condescension involved in caricaturing is so great that it makes having a healthy relationship with such a person very challenging.

Practice exercise: reflective listening with respect

For each of the following statements, fill in the blanks to help you practice listening with respect. Try to use a variety of tentative statements. As with listening with empathy, it doesn't matter if you get the thought exactly correct. What matters is you make an attempt to understand. I have purposely tried to create this exercise so that, whatever your current world view is, you will find statements that you might strongly disagree with and might even create some intense emotional reactions within you. Hang in there; we are going to talk about those reactions after the practice exercise.

1. Your daughter comes to you and says: *I think I'm going to take the next semester off from school. I enjoy my major, but I've been working on my novel and I think it's pretty good. I'd like to spend some concentrated time trying to finish it. Besides, I think the experience of really trying to write a book will make me a much better student when I go back to finish my major in creative writing.*

Identify the thought:

Reflect the thought back to the speaker in a tentative statement:

Identify the value behind the thought:

Reflect the value back to the speaker in a tentative sentence:

Affirm the value:

2. A friend at work says: *It doesn't matter what you believe about God as long as you're sincere. My relationship with God is a personal thing. I'd rather spend Sundays on my own than spend it in church with a bunch of hypocrites who don't really walk their talk anyway.*

Identify the thought:

Reflect the thought back to the speaker in a tentative statement:

Identify the value behind the thought:

Reflect the value back to the speaker in a tentative sentence:

Affirm the value:

3. You're talking to a stranger at the local sports bar and he says: *I would never marry someone unless I lived with her for a while. I wouldn't want to find out that we are not compatible and be stuck being married. It's better to learn that you are not compatible for whatever reason and just move out rather than have to go through a divorce, like my parents did.*

Identify the thought:
Want to be sure about marriage

Reflect the thought back to the speaker in a tentative statement:

Identify the value behind the thought:

marriage is an important thing

Sounds like you want to make sure your marriage will work well

Reflect the value back to the speaker in a tentative sentence:

Affirm the value:

4. You're discussing your summer plans with a friend and he says: *My wife and I are taking our kids on a mission trip to Haiti through our church. We're going to be helping to build a new school. So much of what Jesus talked about in the gospels was God's heart for the poor, and we want to help our kids understand what that really means.*

Identify the thought:

Reflect the thought back to the speaker in a tentative statement:

Identify the value behind the thought:

Reflect the value back to the speaker in a tentative sentence:

Affirm the value:

Mental Barriers and Bad Habits

Some of the sentences in the above exercise might have been a challenge for you, not because you *couldn't* write a reflective sentence, but because everything in you cringed at doing so. We have some serious mental barriers that prevent us from even *wanting* to treat others with respect, and we also have some bad habits that stand in the way of respectful conversation. Let's look at some of these.

It's not about you!

One of the biggest obstacles in listening with respect is to remember that when you are listening to someone then the conversation, at that moment, is about *them* and not about *you*. I've noticed that one of the biggest barriers to listening with respect is when the speaker says something that the listener disagrees with then the listener feels compelled to voice their difference immediately.

Speaker: Disneyland is my favorite place to spend a day off.
Listener: I hate Disneyland. It's so phony.

Speaker: I'm in the mood for an iced coffee.
Listener: Ugh. Iced coffee is horrible. How can you drink that?

Speaker: I think LeBron James is the most talented basketball player ever.
Listener: LeBron is nothing compared to Michael Jordan. LeBron is not even in the top ten all time.

Remember that Stage One of relationship building is about maintaining equal power and value of each person in the relationship. Each person is allowed to have their own thoughts, beliefs, feelings, values, tastes, hopes and dreams. When someone else is talking, if you let your listening be about them then you will show that you have the ability to see them as a separate person who you want to get to know by paying attention to their thoughts, beliefs, opinions, and tastes.

It's not about standing up for God or for the truth

Okay. It's one thing to respect differences in tastes in music or food or movies. It's one thing to respect differences in political views or which football team will win the Super Bowl this year. But what if someone expresses a view that is clearly in opposition to what the Bible teaches. If we listen with respect isn't that the same thing as condoning a falsehood? Isn't it our job to correct them?

Actually, no, it's not our job to correct them. The Apostle Peter is very clear about what our job is when it comes to talking about our faith:

But in your hearts revere Christ as Lord. Always be prepared to give an answer to everyone who asks you to give the reason for the hope that you have. But do this with gentleness and respect. (1 Peter 3:15)

One of the most ignored phrases of scripture is that little phrase "to everyone who asks." Peter assumes that people will be asking Christians why their lives are filled with so much hope. Others will notice the difference and want to know the reason. Peter tells us to be ready, but he doesn't tell us to force our views or opinions on others when they are unwanted. In fact, he says that even if people ask us to share our faith with them, that we must be gentle and respectful while doing so.

I have searched through the New Testament and cannot find an instance in which the early followers of Jesus expressed their faith in a rude or disrespectful manner. Read through the book of Acts and you will notice that each time the disciples expressed their faith they did it in ways that were socially appropriate. Sometimes they were asked questions. Sometimes a miracle had just occurred and the people gathered wanted an explanation. Sometimes they were invited as guest speakers in a synagogue. Sometimes they were brought before judges and asked to explain the reasons for their behaviors. Even when Paul spoke at the marketplace in Corinth, he was following a normal and respectful social behavior. It was the custom for different philosophers and teachers to take turns presenting their views while others listened and debated. Paul simply took his turn.

There is no way to genuinely present the story of God's love in ways that are rude, arrogant and disrespectful. Not only that, but others are much more likely to invite you to share what you believe with them if they have experienced nothing but respect, curiosity and an eagerness to understand when they have shared their thinking with you.

Two impulses

It seems to me as I read the New Testament that there are two different impulses that are meant to guide us in two different arenas. One is an outward impulse; the other is an inward impulse. The outward impulse is that we are to communicate love and respect to every person that we meet, no matter what their beliefs, lifestyles and moral choices. The inward impulse is that, having been forgiven and adopted into the family of God, we are to examine our own beliefs, lifestyles and moral choices and seek to get all the help and grace and truth we need to live lives that are pleasing to God. I think in the church we often mix these two different impulses up: we end up critiquing other people's lives and telling them how far off of God's will it is, and we are satisfied with accepting our own unhealthy behaviors and give no thought to all the areas in which we need to grow and become more whole.

Moving from Respect to Empathy

Sometimes when you are listening with respect you will observe that some emotional content starts to creep in. This happens when the ideas talked about start to connect with something that the speaker loves. When this happens you can move to listening with empathy.

Speaker: I'm thinking a beach vacation would be a good idea this year. I know we wanted to go Europe, but I don't think it's in the budget.

Listener: So it sounds like you think a beach vacation would be more financially responsible. [Listening with respect]

Speaker: Yeah. Honestly, I know I was excited about going to Europe, but every time I think about how expensive it would be when we already have so many financial challenges popping up I get so anxious that planning the vacation doesn't sound like any fun at all.

Listener: So the idea of going to Europe this year is actually causing you a lot of stress, is that right? [Listening with empathy]

Speaker: Yes, it is. And when I thought about just going to the beach and relaxing for a whole week, then I started to get excited about taking a vacation again.

Listener: It sounds like a more affordable and more relaxing vacation this year really gives you not only peace of mind but also something energizing to look forward to. [Listening with empathy]

As you become more practiced at listening with empathy and listening with respect it will be easy to spot when it's time to move from one to the other.

13 Respect and Humility

*Let the wise listen and add to their learning, and let the
discerning get guidance—*
Proverbs 1:5

Humility and respect have a symbiotic relationship. They feed one another. The more you have a proper humility the easier it will be to respect others. And the more you respect others the more you will demonstrate a proper humility towards life. Here is an axiom I believe is helpful in discovering a humble stance towards life. It also helps me enter into conversations with more respect:

I don't know what I don't know.

That's a deceptively simple statement. It seems obvious and almost useless, until you think about the implications. Here is the first implication:

Since I don't know what I don't know, I don't know how much I don't know.

Think about that for a moment. Take any subject that is important to you: God, your spouse, your child, astrophysics, leadership, gardening – anything. Now draw a circle that represents all that can be known about that subject. What happens if you try to turn that circle into a pie chart representing how much of your subject you already know? Would you put your current knowledge of that subject at 5% or 95%? Would you put it at 50%? The reality is, you have no way to accurately draw that chart, because although you know what you know, you don't know what you don't know and you don't know how much you don't know. In other words, you don't know the *volume of learning* that is still available to you.

Here is another implication:

Since I don't know what I don't know, I don't know what new learning will change everything I do know.

People knew quite a bit about astronomy before Copernicus, but his discovery that our solar system was heliocentric caused a realignment of everything that was known in astronomy up until then. People knew a lot about physics before Einstein's theory of relativity, but his discovery not only gave a new context to everything that was known up to that point, it created the possibility for many more discoveries. People knew a lot about manufacturing before Deming and his associates pioneered statistical process control, but once they did it revolutionized mankind's capacity to create higher and higher quality products.

This kind of learning can also happen on a personal level. When parents of a "problem child" learn that he has ADD it can change the way they view their child. They go back through the rolodex of memories of all of the struggles they have had with a new perspective and new way of interpreting the experiences. Before Paul was an apostle he was a Pharisee. And, like any good Pharisee, he knew the Old Testament backwards and forwards. But, after his encounter with Jesus on the road to Damascus, his understanding of everything he read in the Old Testament was changed. We have all had that "this changes everything" experience where we have learned something that not only added to our knowledge set, it completely rearranged and added depth to what we already knew. Because you don't know what you don't know, you don't know what *revolutionary learning* is still available to you.

Here is a third implication:

Since I don't know what I don't know, I don't know how much better my life could be if only I knew what I don't know.

Every once in a while we discover a new truth that not only revolutionizes the way we think, it significantly impacts an area of our life for the better. It probably wouldn't take you too long to think of something you learned that transformed your relationships, your emotional or physical health, your finances, your leadership, or your career. What would your life be like now if you had never learned that one transformative idea? Because you don't know what you don't know, you don't know the *transformative learning* that is waiting to be discovered.

Know-it-alls and Learn-it-alls

We seem to begin life wanting to learn all we can. I can remember the barrage of questions my children hit me with every day when they were little. "Why doesn't the moon fall down? Why are bananas yellow? How far away is Australia? Where do babies come from?" They were unrelenting. When we are young, not knowing something is as natural as breathing, and having the posture of a learner holds no stigma. We want to learn it all. As we journey to adulthood we are all in danger of morphing from learn-it-alls to know-it-alls.

When we take the posture of a know-it-all, we assume that no new learnings will add significantly to the *volume* of what we know, *revolutionize* what we know, or *transform* our lives in significant ways. Because of this, know-it-alls and learn-it-alls enter into conversations with very different mind-sets.

- Know-it-alls believe that their identity and worth come from being right; learn-it-alls believe they are still worthwhile even when they are wrong or uninformed.

- Know-it-alls believe that conversations are chances to show how much they know or to prove that they are right; learn-it-alls believe that conversations are chances to learn things they don't already know or learn where they have been wrong.

- Know-it-alls believe "My opinion and perspective are important because they are mine. To challenge my perspective is to challenge me". Learn-it-alls believe "I am different from my opinions and perspectives. I can change them without losing my value."

- Know-it-alls believe that discovering that they've been wrong is so painful that they avoid conversations where they could discover that they've been wrong. Learn-it-alls believe that discovering that they've been wrong is so helpful and life-changing that they seek out conversations where they can discover that they've been wrong.

You can choose to be a know-it-all or a learn-it-all, but the reality is you don't know what you don't know. Because this is true, only learn-it-alls have an orientation towards reality. When you accept the implications of the fact that you don't know what you don't know, then you can enter into conversations, even with people who are very different from you, not with a resigned humility, but with an eager and thirsty humility. What might you discover in this conversation that you didn't know? How might that change life for the better?

Personal Reflection

Do you think the people in your life would describe you more as a know-it-all or a learn-it-all? What specific behaviors of yours would cause them to make this choice?

What is one specific thing you can do to become more of a learn-it-all in the conversations you have with others this week, even with those who are quite different from you?

14 Respect and Hearing "No"

It's easy to love people when they want what we want, and it's easy to love people if they say Yes to what we want. It's more difficult to love people when they want something different and so choose to say No to what we want. I heard a song recently where the gist of the lyrics was "If you don't do want I want there are four or five women who are eager to take your place within the hour." The power dynamics this guy was looking for in the relationship are very clear: "I'm the only one who gets to want, and I'm the only one who gets to choose. You can't want something different, and you certainly aren't allowed to say No to me."

This might be a great way to live if you are a narcissist, but not if you want to develop healthy relationships. In fact, the ability to not only hear No but to also respect and value No is perhaps the most empowering and life-enhancing ability to develop if you want to love people well.

I was coaching a young man recently in his attempt to find a romantic relationship. He was dating a woman whom he had really fallen for, and he was beginning to wonder if she was "the one." Then one day he asked her to be his girlfriend and she said No. He already knew that she was entering the military in two months and that she was very excited about it. She told him this was a time in her life that she wanted to focus on her career, and she didn't want a serious commitment to anyone until her career was established. He was devastated. This definitely wasn't what he wanted. All he could think about was how to change her No into a Yes. He asked me if he should give her an ultimatum: "Make me your first commitment or I don't want anything to do with you." As we talked about his options he realized that if he wanted to put himself first he could give her an ultimatum, but if he wanted to love her well he could make another choice. He could tell her that he thinks she is a strong, smart woman who knows what she wants out of life, and she should go for it with everything she has in her. He could tell her he was glad they had built such a great friendship and he was eager to stay friends. He could let her know he was disappointed about things not getting more serious, but that was his problem and he would deal with it. If he had chosen to put himself first he would be attempting to make this woman less powerful, less of who she wanted to be. But because he chose the other path, he acknowledged and celebrated her power, and took another step in building a great friendship.

Attacking No

None of us particularly likes hearing No, and because of that we may have developed techniques that we use to try to turn someone's No into a Yes. Sometimes we attack their No overtly. We might demand that they give us reasons for their No:

Why don't you want to go to Florida for vacation? Everybody loves Florida!

You don't want to take the promotion? Why not? It doesn't make sense!

You can't help me move Saturday? What are you doing that's more important?

Not only can we demand an explanation, we can demand that the explanation makes sense not just to *them* but to *us*. Another way we can attack someone's no is to attack their character.

You don't want to have sex? Are you some kind of prude?
You won't fix my car? Are you that selfish?

We can also attack someone's No in a way that is more subtle or passive. We might accept their No but withdraw affection or act distant. We might accept their No but not answer their phone calls for the next three weeks. This is done with the purpose of teaching them a lesson: there is a price to pay if you say No to me.

Let's talk about one of the things that makes hearing No so tricky, and then we'll talk about why it is so critical to develop the ability to respect another person's No.

Hearing No and the grief process

Whenever we hear No we experience a loss. The young man dating the woman going into the military experienced a loss – his hope that this young lady would become his girlfriend and perhaps someday even his wife. If your young son asks you if he can go to the movies and you say No he has experienced a loss, especially if it's a movie he was really excited about seeing, or if seeing it on opening night with his friends held a special meaning to him.

The only way we have of dealing with a loss is to grieve it, and we know that grieving has some predictable stages to it. It always involves denial, anger, bargaining, depression and finally acceptance. If the loss is great (like the death of a loved one, or someone saying No to your marriage proposal) the grief process can be intense. But even smaller losses (like breaking your favorite coffee cup or someone saying No to babysitting for you) can create similar emotional reactions in us, though not so intense. If you have a difficult time respecting someone's No, you are probably getting stuck in the grief process, or trying to escape having to grieve by turning their No into a Yes. If you tend to attack someone's No overtly, you might be getting stuck in the denial, anger or bargaining phase of grieving. If you tend to attack someone's No more passively, you might be getting stuck in the depression stage of letting go.

By the way, when your children get angry or sad when you say No they are not being selfish or spoiled, they are grieving. If you condemn them for their emotional reaction you are asking them to bury their hearts and not love something so much that they would have to grieve its loss. On the other hand, if you placate them by giving in before they get to the acceptance stage they will not be able to practice grieving. If you allow them to finish the grieving process and get to acceptance you will be doing them a huge favor, because they will be much more apt to become adults who can respect another person's No.

The grieving process is natural and unavoidable, so having an emotional reaction when we hear No is not a problem. But here is the key if you want to love others well: You need to see your grief as your problem, not the problem of the person who said No. People who can hear No and say to themselves "Wow, that really hurts" or "I'm angry about that" or "That's really disappointing" but at the same time say to themselves "and that's my problem to deal with" are the kind of people who are able to respect another's No and love them well.

In fact, here is a something to shoot for if you want to enter the major leagues of loving well. Sometimes you might notice someone changing their No to a Yes solely because they see they've disappointed you. Here is a chance to get what you want, but that is a short term win. If instead you can say "That's okay, my disappointment is my problem, and I'm strong enough to handle it. I really want to honor and respect that you said No," then you can achieve a long term win.

The power of No

To understand why that is a long term win we need to understand why No is such an important word, which brings us to another axiom to live by if you want to use your heart to love others well:

When you respect someone's No you protect their Yes

William Ury points out in *The Power of a Positive No* (a book that I think is a must-read for everyone) that when people say No to one thing, it's always because they want to say Yes to something that is more important to them. The young woman going into the military said No to a serious dating relationship because she wanted to say Yes to her career. This was a defining moment. It was an opportunity to see how important serving in the Armed Forces was to her. It was a central part of who she saw herself to be as a person.

When someone says No to working overtime it's because he is not only saying Yes to attending his son's soccer game, he is saying Yes to being involved in his son's life and Yes to being a good father. When someone says No to lending you money to solve your current crisis she is saying Yes to saving for her daughter's college fund. When your wife says No to going to a late movie with you she is not only saying Yes to a good night's sleep, she is also saying Yes to a healthy, balanced, lower-stressed life.

When you understand that someone's No always protects their Yes, you can begin to see their No as a way to glimpse what is most important to them, what their unique passions and dreams and goals are in life. Respecting No is not only a way to understand their uniqueness, it's a way to protect and nurture it.

Whenever I speak about respecting No to groups someone invariably asks "But what about negotiation? Isn't it okay to negotiate a No to a Yes?" It is a great question, and perhaps that is what you have been wondering. If so, I want to remind you that we are working on Stage One skills, which are foundational to loving others well. Healthy negotiation can only happen when both parties are free to say No to the negotiation. If you do not learn first to respect someone's No, negotiation skills will not help you to love well, they will only help you to attack someone's No more skillfully.

Because No is so important, here is another axiom that is helpful to live by if you want to love other's well:

"No." is a complete sentence

In other words, people don't owe you an explanation for their No. They don't have to defend their No to you. Others may choose to explain why they say No, but that is their choice. If they choose not to, respectful people do not press. If the people in your life know that they can say No to you and you will respect it and not demand an explanation, they will get the sense that you see them as a separate person with equal value and equal power.

There is one exception to this, and that is when you believe that the other person is unclear what they are saying No to, for example:

You: Hey honey, our annual corporate dinner is a week from Tuesday, and I really want you to come.

Them: Sorry. I'm just too swamped this time of year, and you know Tuesdays are my worst nights.

You: Yes, I know Tuesday is a bad night and I want to be respectful of that, but my college roommate is going to be there and I was really hoping the two of you could meet.

or

Yes, I know Tuesday is a bad night and I want to be respectful of that, but Mike Matheny is giving the speech, and I know you are a huge Cardinals fan.

Sometimes we might think that someone doesn't understand how important the thing they are saying No to is to *us* (as in the college roommate example) or to *them* (as in the Mike Matheny example), and so we want to clarify what we are asking. Then, if they still choose to say No, we can let it drop because we are certain they understand what they are saying No to.

Personal Reflection:

On a scale of 1 (it's the hardest thing in the world) to 10 (it's often painful but I can do it consistently) how easy is it for you to respect and value other people's No? Why do you think that is? What is one thing that would help you move up the scale one point?

What was the last time you tried to argue someone out of their No? How did that impact your relationship?

Red Flag: If someone does not have the capacity to accept, nurture, and even celebrate your right to say No then there is no basis to have a real relationship, since you will always by default be powerless. Someone who demands an explanation for your No that satisfies his or her thinking doesn't really see you as a separate person.

The Hard Stuff

Sometimes we not only struggle accepting someone's No, we also struggle accepting their Yes. But respecting others not only means respecting their freedom to want and choose things that we don't want. It also means respecting their freedom to want and choose things that we think are wrong or harmful.

Sometimes we will disagree with our children's choice for college or a career. Sometimes we will disagree with our sister's choice of whom to marry. Sometimes we will disagree with the way our best friend spends his money. And when this happens we can sometimes attack others' Yes with three times the energy with which we have ever attacked their No. The problem is that attacking their Yes can also do three times the damage to the relationship as attacking their No.

One of my favorite stories in the Bible is the story of the prodigal son. You've probably heard it. A father has two sons, and one of them decides he doesn't want to stay at home and work for his father anymore. Not only that, he decides that he can't wait for his father to die to receive his inheritance, so he asks if he could have his half of his father's fortune so he can go and live the life he wants. The focus of the story is the father's love and acceptance when the son returns home after making a mess of his life and completely wasting his inheritance. But just as amazing in this story is the father's love and acceptance in allowing the son to make his own choice, take his inheritance, and leave. He allows his son to experience the consequences of poor choices so he can ultimately discover what is important. And when the son returns there is no "I told you so!" or "If you had only listened to me in the first place this wouldn't have happened."

I believe that God is very clear about the choices he would like for us to make. But because God has created us to be separate, valuable, powerful people, he gives each one of us the freedom to choose our own Yes, and to live with consequences of the things to which we say Yes.

Growing in accepting another person's Yes doesn't mean changing your opinions about their Yes. It doesn't mean closing your eyes to the fact that their Yes might end up hurting them. What it means is respecting that they have their own lives to live, that sometimes they might be right and you might be wrong, that when they are wrong they will have to learn from their own mistakes, and that you are going to continue to love and respect them anyway.

Personal Reflection

On a scale of 1 (it's the hardest thing in the world) to 10 (it's often painful but I can do it consistently) how easy is it for you to respect and value other people's Yes if you disagree with it? Why do you think that is? What is one thing that would help you move up the scale one point?

What was the last time you tried to argue someone out of their Yes? How did that impact your relationship?

How to Hear No and Yes respectfully

There are potentially three parts to hearing No well, depending on how the No is delivered. They are:

1. Thank them for answering
2. If appropriate, affirm their Yes
3. If appropriate, take responsibility for your disappointment

1. Thank them for answering.

This can be done in many ways.

Thanks for getting back to me...
I appreciate that quick reply...
Thanks for letting me know your decision...
Thanks for thinking about it...
Thank you for considering it...
Thank you for being honest with me...

2. If appropriate, affirm their Yes.

Sometimes when people say No they do not give an explanation, which is entirely appropriate. If that is the case, then simply thanking them for their answer is enough. Other times they do give an explanation, which is a way of letting you know the Yes that is behind their No. When they do this, it is a great opportunity to show that you value them as separate people who have their own lives to live. You can do this by affirming their Yes.

Them: Sorry, I won't be able to come to your party Saturday night. My brother is coming to town and I want to spend as much time as I can with him.
You: Thanks for getting back to me, that's really helpful. I'm glad you get to spend some time with your brother, I know that's important to you."

Them: I won't be able to help you with your taxes this weekend. My son has a swim meet out of town.
You: Thanks for letting me know that. I really admire how involved you are in your son's life.

3. If appropriate, express responsibility for your disappointment.

Most of the times, the first two steps will be enough to hear No respectfully. Occasionally, you might also need to express responsibility for your disappointment. The only time when this is appropriate is if *the other person* mentions your disappointment or if they express any kind of guilt about causing you pain by saying No. If they don't mention it and *you* bring it up, it will always be perceived as manipulative.

Them: I've given it a lot of thought and I just don't think I'm ready to adopt another child right now. I'm still trying to figure out how to be a good mom to Kendra and Makayla. I feel really badly about that because I know how disappointed you are going to be.

You: Thanks for giving it so much thought, and I really appreciate your honesty. (Thank them for answering). *I don't want to do anything you are not ready for, and I appreciate how important it is for you to focus on being a great mom to our daughters.* (Affirm their Yes) *You're right, I'm really disappointed, but that's my deal and I'll work through it.* (Express responsibility for your disappointment)

Practice Session: Hearing No Respectfully

For each of the following sentences, write out a reply that would communicate your respect for the other person.

1. *I can't babysit for you Thursday. Tom has tickets to the baseball game and it's been forever since we've had a night out.*

2. *I've decided I can't volunteer at the food kitchen. It's a great ministry, but with grad school starting this fall and having a new baby in the house I'm worried that the schedule may already be over-filled.*

3. *Sorry, I'm not free for coffee this Thursday. I might be available next week.*

4. *Mom, Mary and I have decided to stay home for the holidays this year, so we're going to say No to your invitation to spend it with you and Dad. I feel really bad about it because I've never missed Christmas with you and I don't want to hurt your feelings, but this is our first Christmas as a couple and we really want to spend it together at home.*

7. *Thanks for the invitation, but I won't be attending the book club right now.*

6. *I have to say I was really honored when you asked me to go into business with you, but I'm going to have to say No. I've given it a lot of thought and I think I just don't know enough about the health care sector to make that large of an investment.*

Closing Thoughts:

Preparing for Stage Two

15 Reciprocity: Loving and Being Loved

Let no debt remain outstanding, except the continuing debt to love one another, for whoever loves others has fulfilled the law.
Romans 13:8

The main thrust of this book has been learning to love well by developing the attitudes and the skills necessary to protect the other person's value and power as a separate human being. So in a sense, this entire book is about the other person. You may have noticed that there really hasn't been much about you in this book. We haven't covered attitudes or skills necessary to talk about your thoughts or your wants or your desires. Here's why: before you connect with someone, you need to make sure they are a safe and healthy person to connect with. Why would you want to connect with someone who does not have the ability to value you? Why would you want to share your thoughts, opinions, dreams and desires with someone who doesn't have the capacity to respect you as an individual? Why would you want to open your heart to someone who will try to bury it?

You were not only designed to love, you were designed to be loved. Love is the fuel that we run on. You need to be loved well by others if you are going to be all that you were meant to be. But if you allow yourself to get stuck in relationships with people who cannot love well – people who feel justified in making your value negotiable depending on how they feel, or people who want to bury your heart because it is more convenient for them if you don't have feelings, or people who want to take away your power to think and decide for yourself – you will never grow and blossom into the person you could be. Your tank will be empty, and you will experience frustration as you try to be good enough to earn love from people who are not able to give it.

In order to lay a great foundation for a long and satisfying relationship, then, there are two things that are critical. The first is to practice the basic skills we have covered in this book until you have become proficient in them. I cannot overemphasize the importance of this. You cannot become a great basketball player by reading a book about how to play basketball. You have to practice the various dribbling, passing and shooting skills every day until you can do them well without thinking about them.

The second thing you need to do is to stop trying to make people love, value, and respect you. That is not your job. You do not have that much power or control. Your job is to listen to, value and respect others, then *pay attention to who has the desire and ability to listen to, value and respect you in return.* These are the people with whom you will want to move into Stage Two. These are the people that you will want to connect with. This leads to another axiom of loving well:

Reciprocity: Only move on to Stage Two (Creating Connection) of relationship building when BOTH people are exhibiting the attitudes and practicing the skills of Stage One (Loving Well).

Whenever I present this material to a group I invariably hear questions like "How can I make this person respect my No?" or "What can I do to make this person be more warm towards me?" The answer is you cannot make them do anything. You can suggest it. You can let the people you want to have relationship with know how important it is to you. You can offer to work through this book together with them. But you cannot make them change.

So what do you do with those funny, brilliant, attractive, fun, exciting people that despite all their wonderful qualities consistently bury your heart, devalue and disrespect you? You have a choice to make, but here is something that I have found to be true:

In relationships, you don't get what you need. You don't get what you want. You don't get what is fair. You don't get what you deserve. In relationships, you get what you tolerate. You get what you put up with.

If you stop tolerating devaluing and disrespectful behavior, then the people who want to use you will tend to leave. Make a decision that you are going to limit how much of your heart you give to people who do not want to do the hard work of loving well.

Dating

If you are currently dating and want someone to share your life with, this can be very helpful. Often we have two ideas running through our minds while dating that make it a very stressful experience: Are they the one I want? And if they are, am I the one they want? Another way to say this is: Are they good enough for me and am I good enough for them? This leads to a host of other questions: Do they want to get married? Do they want kids? Are they attractive? Am I attractive enough for them? Do they make enough money? Do I make enough money? Are my jokes funny enough? Do they think I'm fun? And on and on.

Do you notice what all of these questions have in common? They are all evaluation questions. We go out on dates and we try to have fun with someone we are evaluating and who we believe is evaluating us, and what is at stake is the deepest desire of our hearts. No wonder many people avoid dating. It's like trying to combine a party with a job interview for your dream job. Have you ever looked forward to a job interview?

Let me invite you to change your approach to dating. Instead of seeing it as an opportunity to find a potential spouse, see it as an opportunity to begin to get to know another human being. Use it as an opportunity to find out who they are and what makes them tick, how they think and how they feel about life. See them as valuable people in and of themselves regardless of whether or not they can do anything for you. This shift of approach is helpful for several reasons. First of all, it is doable! Every date can be a success because if you use the skills you have learned in this book you can begin to get to know someone on every date you go on. Secondly, you will create the opportunity to find a lot of great friendships with people you have no intention of marrying. If you go on a date with an all or nothing mindset, you almost always get nothing. Finally, you will be able to relax and be the real you because you are not concerned with impressing the other person, just getting to know them.

You can do the same thing in other social environments besides dating: at a party, at work, in a Bible study at church, at the sports bar watching the big game. Begin looking for lots of opportunities simply to get to know people. Make it your goal to get to know a little bit about fifty different people in the next year, simply by listening to them with empathy and respect. If you do this you will discover that there may be five or ten of those conversations that you really enjoyed, and that the other person also showed interest in getting to know you.

It is not your job to find the right person and try to get them to fall in love with you. You don't have that much power. Your job is to listen to, value and respect others and *pay attention to who listens to, values and respects you in return.* These are the people you will want to try to create a deeper connection with, and it will be a less stressful experience because you already know they have the capacity to listen to you, value you, and respect you as a separate human being.

Parents

Parents, it is absolutely critical that you understand the importance of reciprocity. The best thing you can do for your children is to teach them the skills and attitudes that are essential to be able to love well. Yes, this will help them to be better friends. But just as importantly it will help them to choose better friends. They will be much less likely to grow up and choose friends or a spouse who is disrespectful or controlling or self-absorbed because they will see the red flags a mile away. They will be more apt to choose relationships with people who can give love and receive love freely. There are not many things you could do for your children that will have a bigger impact on their happiness and well-being.

And the best way to do this is to start loving them well right now. Spend time listening to them and helping them excavate their hearts. Validate their feelings so that they learn to take their hearts seriously and learn how to protect and nurture their relationships with the people and things they love. Treat them with warmth always, and show appreciation to them on a regular basis. And make sure you are giving them the appropriate respect at each stage of their journey into adulthood.

Marriage

For marriage to have any kind of romance or passion, there needs to be two separate, valuable, powerful people in the relationship. You cannot have any fireworks with one strong person and one weak person. Sometimes relationships that started out as exciting and fun in the dating stage (when it was clear that there were two separate people) stagnate as time goes by because the partners fail to practice the behaviors that protect each other's value and power. Sometimes this happens because one person wants more control. But it can also happen because one person wants no control – they would prefer having someone else to blame for their unhappiness and act like a victim rather than doing the hard work of taking responsibility for their lives. However it happens, a marriage that has lost the sense that there are two different people who each have equal value and power can be lifeless.

The good news is that the original passion and romance of the dating phase of the relationship can be recaptured. Marriages that have turned into drudgery can be reignited by couples who have decided to take each other's emotional worlds seriously, communicate value through warmth and appreciation, and listen to one another's thoughts, opinions, dreams, wants, and tastes with respect. And marriages that are already stable can become even stronger and more rewarding by working through the practices in this book together. When you master these skills, you create the safe and accepting environment that is essential for deep connection to take place.

Church Leaders

One of the great things that has happened in the church over the past 30 years or so is a heightened awareness of the importance of authentic community. Small groups especially have been seen as a vehicle for recapturing the biblical ideal of loving one another deeply. I'm a big supporter of small groups, but they can have a fatal flaw: they only produce authentic Christian community if the people in the group know how to love well. And sadly, it can only take one person telling others what they should or shouldn't feel, or one person acting like a know-it-all, or one person fixing others by quoting Scripture at them instead of empathizing with their pain, and suddenly what could have been a great experience of community has become another duty to endure. And quite often, the person who is preventing the real community from taking place can be the most spiritual-sounding person of the group. They are always on God's side telling us how we should think or feel or behave.

When we ignore the importance of reciprocity and ask our church members to create connection with people who are not able to love well in return, we are creating situations that can actually damage church members emotionally and spiritually. If you are a church leader, one of the best things you can do for your church is to model the practices and attitudes of loving well, and make them standard operating procedure in your church. Teach them to your leadership team and ensure that you are listening to one another with empathy and validation, and that you are consistently treating one another with value and respect. Teach them to your small group leaders and help them create safe groups where each person knows that they are going to be loved well. Decide today that, whatever else you get wrong as a spiritual leader, you are not going to get loving one another wrong.

16 Loving God Well

*Therefore, if you are offering your gift at the altar and there
remember that your brother or sister has something against you,
leave your gift there in front of the altar. First go and be
reconciled to them; then come and offer your gift.
Matthew 5:23-24.*

This statement by Jesus in the above quote is remarkable. Imagine you are a Jew living in that time period and you have come to offer your gift at the temple in Jerusalem. Perhaps you have come from somewhere in Judea or from up north in Galilee. Perhaps you have come from Rome or Corinth or Alexandria. Wherever you have come from, this is a big day for you. You started the day with the ceremonial cleansing required for anyone entering into the temple. You have stood for hours in a throng of people and have finally entered into the court of gentiles, only to meet another mass of people at the money changers' table, where you change your money into the currency of the temple. Then you take your temple money and enter another line to purchase an offering gift that has been certified by the priests as blameless and acceptable. Finally you are at the altar ready to give your gift to God. You hear the temple music playing and smell the aroma of the sacrifices being burnt all around you and are aware that you are coming into the presence of God in a unique and special way – certainly one of the most anticipated and holy moments of your year if not your lifetime. And Jesus says, when you are in that holy moment, if you remember that you have harmed someone in any way, leave your gift in front of the altar – leave that sacred moment of connection with God, and go and make things right with the person first. He doesn't say to make a mental note to do it later when it is convenient, but to do it right then.

I would have thought Jesus' priority would have been the other way around: Get your relationship with God right first and then you will be in a position to get your relationship with others right. But he teaches just the opposite. Why does he do this? I think it is to help us sidestep a misconception that will always lead to huge barrier in growing in our ability to love God well.

The misconception is that it is easier to love God well than it is to love others well. It's an easy misconception to buy into: after all, God is loving us perfectly, so our relationship with Him must be better than all the others! And it's an easy step from this idea to the notion that the reason that our relationships with others are so strained is because they don't understand us the way God does, or they don't appreciate us the way God does, or they don't see our true motives the way God does. If only other people were as perfect as God, our relationships with them would be just as good. The apostle John, perhaps Jesus' closest friend among all his disciples, understood how critical it is to eradicate this misconception. In one of his letters he writes:

For whoever does not love their brother and sister, whom they have seen, cannot love God, whom they have not seen. (1 John 4:20)

John is pointing out that learning to love God well is not easier than learning to love others well, it is actually more difficult. And the reason is obvious: God is invisible. We don't get the immediate feedback when we are talking to Him. We can't ask him "God, how am I doing at loving you well?" and hear Him say that we seem distracted when we talk to Him, or that we seem emotionally detached, or that He wishes our conversations weren't so self-absorbed. We can't see his body language or facial expressions. And in the absence of this feedback we tend to imagine what God's response is, and we usually tend to imagine that God sees things just the way we do. God is just as passive or co-dependent or rage-filled or apathetic as we are. What we do, in reality, is turn God into our imaginary friend. An imaginary friend who generally sees things our way, takes our side, and wonders with us why everyone else doesn't see how right we are.

Jesus is having none of that, and neither is John. They will not allow us to turn God into an imaginary friend. They force us to focus on how well we love others as the litmus test of how well we are able to love God.

Here is the sober truth: God probably experiences you the same way everyone else experiences you. If most people experience you as emotionally shut down, then that is how God probably experiences you. If most people experience you as self-absorbed, then that is how God probably experiences you. If others generally experience you as cold, or passive, or opinionated, or rude, or abrupt, or unappreciative, or afraid of intimacy, or undefined then that is probably how God experiences you as well.

God loves us perfectly, but the barriers that prevent us from having a deeper relationship with God are all on our side. Because God is invisible, we cannot tell what those barriers are just by being in relationship with God. The only way we are going to discover and correct our relational shortcomings is in our relationships with other men and women. Once we have discovered where we are struggling to love other people well, then we know what we need to practice. As we practice the skills and change our attitudes to become more loving with one another, we will become people who can have a healthier connection with God as well.

And I'm not going to let you off the hook on this one, so don't think about that one person you have a great relationship with because they agree with you on everything. Think about the last fifty to a hundred people you have interacted with: Friends, colleagues, children, parents, church members, customers, cashiers, waiters, nurses, teachers or classmates. How many of them would describe you as warm and appreciative? Think about the last fifty to a hundred people you have had conversations with: How many of them would describe you as respectful and interested in really knowing them as individuals? Think about the last fifty to a hundred people who tried to share their emotional world with you: How many of them would describe you as empathetic and understanding? The more you can push the percentage up in your answers to these questions, the greater your capacity to love God well will become.

In this book we have focused on seeing others as separate people with their own value and power. When we think about God's separateness we are approaching what theologians refer to as God's holiness.

"For my thoughts are not your thoughts, neither are your ways my ways," declares the Lord. "As the heavens are higher than the earth, so are my ways higher than your ways and my thoughts than your thoughts." Isaiah 55:8-9.

It takes time, attention, and humility to understand and relate to other people, but much more to understand a transcendent, divine being. Let's review the three major parts of this book to see how developing the skills to love others well might help you lay a foundation for a better relationship with God.

Living with your heart alive: God is not an idea; He is a personal, all-loving being. As a personal, all-loving being He has emotions. In your relationship with God, do you pay attention to His feelings? Are you aware of His anger towards human trafficking or racism or exploitation of the poor and defenseless? Are you aware of how extreme poverty breaks His heart? Are you aware of His intense longing to have a relationship with every man and woman on earth? Do you see the desperate passion that allowed him to offer his only Son's life so that He could offer salvation to all without compromising his justice and holiness? Can you empathize with His elation when one prodigal son or daughter returns home to embrace a relationship with his or her heavenly Father? Do you ask Him to reveal to you His heart towards your city, or how He feels about what is happening in your life or your friendships or your career? God's emotions are always about something that He loves, and if we want to love God well we will take His emotions seriously.

Protecting others' value: In your relationship with God do you remember that genuineness is about you and warmth is about Him? Are you able to consistently express warmth towards God in the midst of asking for what you need or expressing your own pain and confusion? Or do you tend to take Him for granted? Do you show appreciation to God on a regular basis? Do you remember to tell God in concrete language the specific things He has done that you are thankful for, and what difference they are making in your life, and how you can see how this gift is an example of His love or mercy or creativity or brilliance or patience or gentleness?

Protecting others' power: Are you aware that God is not only different than you, He is utterly different than you? Are you aware that His thoughts are not your thoughts, and that it might take time and attentiveness to understand what He has revealed about Himself, both in His works and His word? Do you try to understand God's thinking or do you tend to caricature or minimize or ignore anything that you don't immediately agree with? Are you aware that, when it comes to who God is and what He is doing and what His will is, you don't know what you don't know? Do you open the Bible regularly to learn something about God that you don't already know? Are you aware that you might learn something new today that will make you think: "I knew God was good, but I never understood He was *that* good!"? Do you love God's No as much as you love His Yes? Do you try to see how God's No is always trying to protect a higher Yes?

In the next two books we will talk about how to connect deeply with God and how to share an intimate journey with God to accomplish great things together, but we can't get the cart before the horse. In our relationship with God, just as in our relationship with men and women, we can tend to try to skip the "loving well" stage and head straight to the "connecting deeply" stage or even the "sharing the journey" stage. But it doesn't work. God understands the importance of reciprocity to a great relationship, and though he always goes first, he will wait for you to catch up before moving to the next stage.

And how do we develop the skills to love God well? By learning to love one another well. And that takes work and practice. I want to invite you to keep practicing the skills in this book until you have mastered them, until they are so natural to you that you do them without thinking. When you have mastered the skills necessary to love others well and protect their separate value and power as unique individuals, you will also be able to love God well and create the foundation for a truly intimate relationship with Him.

Notes

Chapter 1

[1]I first heard these very helpful ideas about the meaning of happiness, sadness, fear and anger on one of the Monday Night Solutions tapes by Dr. Henry Cloud & Dr. John Townsend. The tape was loaned to me by a friend over ten years ago, and unfortunately I don't remember the name of it, or if it was Dr. Cloud or Dr. Townsend who was speaking that evening. But it was one of those "hit by lightning" experiences that changed my life and I have never forgotten it. The reason the speaker calls these our primary emotions is because these are the emotions experienced both by humans and by God. I highly recommend the resources available at cloudtownsend.com.

Chapter 4

[1] One example of Jesus' anger occurs in a confrontation with the Pharisees.

Then Jesus asked them, "Which is lawful on the Sabbath: to do good or to do evil, to save life or to kill?" But they remained silent. He looked around at them in anger and, deeply distressed at their stubborn hearts, said to the man, "Stretch out your hand." He stretched it out, and his hand was completely restored. (Mark 3:4-5)

Jesus anger was a signal to him that something he loved was being attacked and needed to be protected. In this case people that he loved needed to be protected from the hard hearted teachers who were out of touch with God's priorities.

We get a picture of Jesus's sadness as he nears the city of Jerusalem.

As he approached Jerusalem and saw the city, he wept over it. (Luke 19:41)

The Greek word translated *wept* in this passage means to wail or to sob convulsively. Jesus models for us what it means to grieve. Here Jesus is losing something that he loved dearly, a relationship with Jerusalem as provider and protector, and the only response was to grieve. Jesus embraced his sorrow and did not try to cover it up with trite sayings or superficial clichés.

In the garden of Gethsemane we also see Jesus' ability to feel both sorrow and fear

Then Jesus went with his disciples to a place called Gethsemane, and he said to them, "Sit here while I go over there and pray." He took Peter and the two sons of Zebedee along with him, and he began to be sorrowful and troubled. Then he said to them, "My soul is overwhelmed with sorrow to the point of death. Stay here and keep watch with me." (Matthew 26:36-38)

An angel from heaven appeared to him and strengthened him. And being in anguish, he prayed more earnestly, and his sweat was like drops of blood falling to the ground. (Luke 22:44)

It's hard to imagine a more intense description of sadness and fear than is captured in these two passages. Because Jesus chose to live with his heart alive, he experienced his feelings deeply.

Chapter 9

[1]C.S. Lewis, *The Weight of Glory,* (New York: HarperCollins Publishers, Inc., 2001), 45-46.

To contact the author about speaking or training for your church, organization or event, email him at:

howtouseyourheart@yahoo.com

61418479R00099

Made in the USA
Lexington, KY
14 March 2017